WORK WITH OLDER PEOPLE

WORK WITH OLDER PEOPLE

Challenges and Opportunities

Edited by

IRENE A. GUTHEIL

Fordham University Press
New York
1994

Library of Congress Cataloging-in-Publication Data

Work with older people: challenges and opportunities / edited by
  Irene A. Gutheil.
    p.cm.
    Includes bibliographical references.
    ISBN 0-8232-1506-7 : $25.00.

    1. Social work with the aged—United States. I.
Gutheil, Irene A.
HV1461.W67   1994
362.6'0973—dc20   93–22670
                                       CIP

Printed in the United States of America

FTW
AFD 7877

CONTENTS

Introduction   1
   Irene A. Gutheil

PART I: SETTING THE STAGE

1. Practice with Older Persons: Challenges and
   Opportunities   9
   Barbara Silverstone

2. Developmental Theories in the Second Half of
   Life   29
   Lynn M. Tepper

3. Family Relationships in Later Life   42
   Lynn M. Tepper

PART II: ISSUES IN PRACTICE AND SERVICE DELIVERY

4. Cultural Diversity and Practice with Older People   65
   Elaine Congress and Martha V. Johns

5. Elder Abuse: Policy and Practice for Social
   Workers   85
   Patricia Brownell

6. Social Work and Bioethics: Ethical Issues in
   Long-Term Care Practice   109
   Bart Collopy and Martha C. Bial

7. Interdisciplinary Teams in Geriatric Settings   139
   Eileen R. Chichin and Ilse R. Leeser

8. Case Management: A Pivotal Service in
   Community-Based Long-Term Care   162
   Sally Robinson

9. Impact of the Environment on Agencies Serving
   Older Adults   182
      Roslyn H. Chernesky

Afterword: Aging in the 1990s   212
      Steven R. Gambert

About the Contributors   217

WORK WITH OLDER PEOPLE

Introduction

Irene A. Gutheil

THE NUMBER OF OLDER PEOPLE in the United States is growing far more rapidly than the rest of the population. In sheer numbers, the aged 65 and older cohort is impressive—it is larger than the entire population of Canada (U.S. Senate, 1988). Demographers have predicted that the numbers of persons over 65 years old will increase dramatically, absolutely and as a percentage of the population, during the next 50 years. Today, the elderly represent approximately 12% of the total population of the United States. Current projections indicate that early in the 21st century, when the postwar "baby boom" generation grows old, about one in five Americans will be over 65 years of age. The oldest old, individuals 85 years of age or older, constitute the fastest-growing segment of this country's population (U.S. Senate, 1988). The growth in the number and proportion of older persons is one of the most dramatic and influential developments of this century, and we must anticipate and address the needs of this burgeoning older population.

One anticipated result of the increasing numbers of older persons, especially the oldest old, is an unprecedented demand for support services for older people and their families. Although technological advances may reduce the length of time people experience chronic disability, the incidence of chronic illness and the need for assistance with activities of daily living does increase with age. Approximately 31% of persons over the age of 85 need some assistance with activities of daily living compared to less than 3% of persons 65 to 74 years old (U.S. House of Representatives, 1987).

In addition to demographic trends, changes in family structure such as high divorce rates and the aging of primary caregivers may result in greater reliance on the social service delivery network. As a result of demographic and social trends, policymakers in both the public and the private sectors are grappling with how to prepare for an aging society and how to make the current service delivery system more responsive to the needs of older Americans.

Service providers, too, are struggling with the increasing needs of an aging population. Greater numbers of professionals interested in and trained to work with older people and their families are needed to do this important work.

During their training, relatively few social work students express a specific interest in working in the field of aging. Although it is not entirely clear why this is the case, several factors are believed to contribute. Working with older people is not recognized as the exciting opportunity it actually is. Students do not recognize the tremendous possibilities for personal growth among the older population. Failing to see older people as integrated into families, many students overlook the potential for family treatment and intergenerational practice. The range of clinical modalities for work with older people often goes unrecognized. In addition, some students fear the possibility of coming too close to their own inevitable aging and mortality, a fear they share with others training in the helping professions.

However, even when social workers enter the field with no intention of serving an older population, chances are they will be working with older people at some time during their practice. Many agencies not necessarily seen as targeting older people do in fact serve older clients. The most obvious example is hospitals. Older persons are also served by family service agencies, out-patient mental health clinics, domestic violence programs, and so forth. Often, once out in the world of practice and seeing more and more older clients, social workers feel an increasing need for greater knowledge about working with this age group. This book is intended for both students and practitioners interested in learning about the challenges inherent in practice with older people.

The idea for this book grew out of a conference held at Fordham University's Graduate School of Social Service. The title, *Work with older people: Challenges and opportunities*, reflects the theme of the conference. Work in the field of aging presents many challenges: some frustrating; some invigorating. It also presents many opportunities for stimulating and gratifying practice. The chapters that follow reflect the remarkable diversity of the challenges and opportunities in work with older people. The content of the book is organized into two parts: Setting the Stage and Issues in Practice and Service Delivery. Part I comprises three chapters, providing the foundation essential to work with older people and their families. The six chapters in Part II examine a range of issues that has demanded increasing attention in recent years.

In the first chapter, Barbara Silverstone discusses practice concerns currently confronting us in our work with older people. These relate primarily to impairments of advanced old age, the struggles of caregiving, and the impact of complicated systems of care on social work practice. Silverstone reviews a practice model that can be applied to diverse populations and across varied settings, and addresses the challenges the future elderly will present to us.

Two chapters by Lynn Tepper follow. In the first, Tepper reviews some developmental theories that address the second half of life. In her discussion of growth, change, and life transitions, Tepper describes some common patterns in later life and provides a foundation for understanding development in old age. In the next chapter, Tepper considers the complexity of family relationships in later life. Stressing the importance of viewing older people in the context of their families, Tepper reviews a range of family issues such as parent–adult-child relationships, widowhood, and the impact of dementia. Her discussion of counseling older families emphasizes the tremendous diversity that exists among older people and their families.

Elaine Congress and Martha Johns lead off Part II with a discussion of the increasingly diverse older population and the accompanying challenges to service providers. The authors make the point that the differences in the life experiences of minority older people do not abate with old age, and that obstacles to service delivery and utilization must

be recognized and addressed. Congress and Johns call upon
service providers to become better informed and better
trained to deal with the cultural diversity among the older
population.

Patricia Brownell's chapter addresses elder abuse, an issue of growing concern in the field of aging. Although it has
come into public awareness only relatively recently, elder
abuse is not a new problem. Brownell reviews definitions of
elder abuse, profiles of victims and their abusers, and models of intervention. In closing, Brownell underscores the role
of the social worker in dealing with this problem.

In the next chapter, Bart Collopy and Martha Bial examine ethical issues in long–term-care practice, an area of
bioethics that has, thus far, received only limited attention.
The issues that social workers in long–term-care settings
deal with are diverse and often highly complex. Resolving
one problem may stir up others. Collopy and Bial use several
cases to illustrate ethical problems confronting social workers and provide some road-maps for negotiating the rugged
terrain these practitioners face.

Eileen Chichin and Ilse Leeser write about interdisciplinary teams and their role in helping older people whose
needs have reached a high degree of complexity. The role
and function of interdisciplinary teams are examined as are
some of the difficulties that may arise when two or more
disciplines work closely together. Chichin and Leeser address the role of education in enhancing interdisciplinary
teamwork. An examination of three different teams illustrates teamwork in action.

In the chapter that follows, Sally Robinson considers case
management as a pivotal service in community-based long-
term care. The practice of case management is complex, and
requires that the social worker operate on many levels simultaneously. Robinson addresses issues ranging from client self-determination to accountability, and reviews
mechanisms for improving the case management process.
She underscores the importance of the relationship between
client and case manager.

Roslyn Chernesky writes that agencies serving older people are strongly influenced by the environment in which they operate. This environment determines what services are delivered and to whom. As Chernesky notes, managers and direct service workers are continually being affected. Chernesky examines the aging service delivery network, recent shifts in the environment, and the implications for agencies and workers.

Steven Gambert's afterword reminds us that today's older people are survivors, who may ultimately face complex, often interacting problems. It is time to address the current shortage of professionals who are knowledgeable about the challenges older people face and have the skills to help.

REFERENCES

U.S. House of Representatives. (1987). *Exploding the myths: Caregiving in America.* A study by the Subcommittee on Human Services of the Select Committee on Aging (Comm. Pub. No 99611). Washington, DC: U.S. Government Printing Office.

U.S. Senate. (1988). *Developments in aging: 1987. Vol. 1.* A report of the Special Committee on Aging. Washington, DC: U.S. Government Printing Office.

PART I

Setting the Stage

1

Practice with Older Persons: Challenges and Opportunities

Barbara Silverstone

INTRODUCTION

THE FIELD OF DIRECT PRACTICE with older persons presents something of a quandary, for we are speaking of a client population that includes three to four generations and a broad spectrum of racial and ethnic groups. It is a population that includes individuals with widely differing family configurations, varying abilities and capabilities, and divergent physical, mental, emotional, and social problems. The older population includes individuals who are blessed by economic affluence or cursed by abject poverty; those who can grow and change over the years or who are rigidly fixated in their ways; those who are optimistic about the future; those who are despairing; and those who are dying.

Does this litany sound familiar to you? It should, for we could be talking about any age group in our society. After all, the old of today are the young of yesterday, bringing into later life their widely divergent characteristics. Thus, just as with younger clients, there can be no set list of practice rules and principles to follow in working with them. Work with older persons demands all the ingredients of generic social work practice, from a careful assessment of the individual's biopsychosocial cultural situation to interventions on the levels of individual, family, organizational, and environmental systems. It calls for meeting the client where he or she is, and for collaborating and problem solving in a manner enhancing the client's self-determination. Like work with younger clients, work with older people challenges us to overcome biases within ourselves related to sexism, racism, and ageism.

What stands out in our work with older persons is that it can be even more exciting and challenging than work with younger persons because we are dealing with survivors who have crossed the terrain of the life course, and who bring into old age the richness of experience, and into advanced old age a very special perspective on life, unique psychological mechanisms for preserving a sense of self, and the strength and fragility that result from having lived through multiple and often unremitting losses.

Other differentials *do* exist for social work practice with older persons, but for the most part these differentials are related not so much to the fact of being old as to those problems among the old we have *chosen* to address and to the settings and circumstances in which we address these problems. It is the practice issues related to these problems, settings, and circumstances that I shall discuss here. They do not make up the universe of situations encountered by older persons. Predictions for the future strongly suggest that as the aging population changes we shall have to address a much broader set of problems, and I shall touch on this expectation later. For now, I shall focus on the problems and practice issues that for the most part confront us now.

THE PROBLEMS WE FACE

These problems relate largely to functional disability among the old and their need for long-term care, and, in the case of neglect and abuse, protective services. Given the higher incidence of mental and physical impairment in a rapidly growing very old population, this emphasis is understandable. Millions fill our nursing homes, and there are many others who place inordinate pressures on family and home-care providers for support. (I might note that similar problems are being faced with persons with AIDS.) Long-term care was an overlooked area of concern until recently. It was the professional and consumer communities in the 1970s

and 1980s which successfully brought societal and governmental attention to the crisis in long-term care and the
harsh pressures being placed on families. Sound financial
strategies still elude us, and services are wanting, but the
problem has taken center stage and has become synonymous
with aging issues in both health and human services.

Typical clients among the older populations, therefore,
are persons of advanced age, frail, and chronically functionally disabled, needing supportive and protective care, who
seek or are receiving nursing home care and home-care
services or whose crisis presents itself to the social workers
in case management agencies, protective service, or acute
hospital settings. The social worker's role can include serving as a gatekeeper, discharge planner, and case manager.

A number of compelling issues have emerged for social
work practice with this population in these settings. One
relates to the often helpless condition of our older clients,
resulting from impairment and the exigencies of advanced
old age. Of paramount concern is the fact that they can no
longer care for themselves as a result of physical immobility
and/or mental impairment compounded by severe emotional
reactions and, not infrequently, sensory loss.

Ironically, this is a client population desperately in need
of help and yet the most difficult to help. Sensory difficulties,
particularly hearing loss and mental impairment, as seen in
those with Alzheimer's disease, are roadblocks to communication and to effectively retaining control of their own lives.

This irony plays itself out in the social work relationship
and, of course, impacts heavily on family members. Helping
this population is an awesome challenge to the practitioner's
skill. Client self-determination seems at times an unrealistic
ideal, as the personal autonomy of older clients seems to
dissipate in a system of care which is becoming increasingly
regulatcd, and in which even life-and-death decisions are
taken out of the older person's hands.

Closely related to the difficulties presented by a client
population who are suffering severe depletions and losses is
the role played by their families. Many of them are coping
on a day-to-day basis with frail and impaired elders. Some

are desperately struggling. Some have given up. It is well
documented that family members are truly the long-term
providers of care to the frail and disabled elderly, yet many
are themselves in late life, or are burdened with other
responsibilities. What role can they effectively play as primary caregivers to the elderly or in secondary roles? How do
we address the family's self-determination and the personal
autonomy of each of its members?

Last, but not least, is the overriding issue of the social
worker's autonomy in a system of care that imposes serious
constraints on effective practice. Social workers in hospitals
and long-term and protective care settings are typically
overburdened by large case loads. A host of policies and
procedures constrict or thwart professional efforts.

The hidden or not so hidden agenda of the settings in
which we practice is the disposition, in the most rapid and
presumably least costly manner, of the long–term-care case.
Hospitals are pressured to discharge elderly patients as
quickly as possible, and this action precipitates decisions
about long-term care. Nursing homes, home-care settings,
and case management agencies must keep sharply focused
on providing only the amount of care demanded by the
client's functional impairments. Protective service agencies
are so overwhelmed by numbers that abuse cases seemingly
can be treated only in the most bureaucratic or legalistic
manner.

Funding streams have constricted the services that can be
provided, including social work and rehabilitation services.
In New York State, Medicaid will pay more than $70,000 per
annum per person for nursing home care, yet rehabilitation
that can reduce or prevent functional disability resulting
from impaired hearing, vision, or motor activity is severely
restricted under both Medicaid and Medicare. Little recognition is given to the cost-effectiveness of meaningful social
work intervention that can allay precipitous decisions and
costly plans of care.

This issue, the constraints placed on professional practice
by social and health care policies and administrative proce-

dures, is perhaps the most serious of all, for it impinges on our ability to apply our skills on behalf of frail impaired older people and their families, not only in terms of their need for long-term care, but also in terms of the quality of life and of self-determination to the extent possible.

To address these issues, broad strategies are required, including advocacy on the federal, state, and local levels, to protect the rights of vulnerable older persons, on the one hand, and the professional practice of social work, on the other. I point to such effective measures as the Nursing Home Bill of Rights enacted in some states, and the recent, very successful effort by the National Association of Social Workers and other advocacy groups to retain in the New York State Nursing Home Code requirements for professional social workers, and a broader definition of their professional role.

Also called for are strategies on the level of practice which enable us to intervene effectively with and on behalf of older clients who suffer cognitive and sensory losses, and to appropriately involve and help their families within the severe constraints often placed on professional practice. This is the challenge that faces us now and that will continue to face us in this time of economic uncertainty and severe government cutbacks. Yet, despite these constraints, opportunities for creative practice do exist.

One set of strategies was presented by Dr. Ann Burack-Weiss and me in a model we developed more than ten years ago and described in *Social work practice with the frail elderly and their families: The auxiliary function model* (1983).

The model remains a relevant one, for the issues we addressed then are even more compelling today as the numbers of the very old frail elderly increase and the resources in support of long-term care dwindle. Furthermore, we have discovered that this model has universal applications for younger groups of ailing, frail, and impaired populations—a fact brought home to us by our more recent experiences with the younger disabled and with persons with AIDS.

A Practice Model

The name of the model is based on a metaphor; the image is that of an auxiliary lighting system which is triggered into action by the failure of a permanent system, and fades when power is restored. An auxiliary adds to, fills in for, and bolsters what has been depleted. An auxiliary also retreats when no longer needed. In human terms, we are referring to the role of a significant other in support of a frail, disabled adult.

The auxiliary-function model encompasses both an eco-systems perspective that has proven valuable in conceptualizing the reciprocity of people and their environments and the notion of adaptive fit. To discuss functionally dependent adults without such external references would seem absurd. By the same token, contributions from ego psychology, particularly those having to do with efficacy and competence, are relevant to the frail and impaired, who are usually provided too few opportunities for mastery and the enhancement of self-esteem. Crisis intervention holds a priority position in our model, given the vulnerability of the client group, for whom developmental or situational life events of even a minor nature have potential for immediate and devastating consequences. Incorporated as well are problem-solving and task-oriented models of practice that alert the profession to the importance of focus, direction, and goal-setting, including a mandate for client involvement in planning, too frequently overlooked in cases of frailty and disability.

Each of these contributions to social work theory accents the positive and the productive. That the client can manage his or her own life, if provided with the opportunity and the skill to do so, is currently our belief system in social work. The auxiliary function model of social work practice, however, seeks to modify this course as it relates to frail or temporarily and permanently impaired, and often dying, adults. Unlike with a healthier population, for these adults change is often for the worse, and supportive care may be required. The maintenance of the status quo may also be an appropriate and useful intervention and goal, as well as change for the better. Our practice model seeks to encompass all these situations.

THE AUXILIARY ROLE

Our model addresses the issues I have raised concerning our older client, their families, and the role of social workers primarily through an understanding of and implementation of the auxiliary role.

The auxiliary role is predicated on the depletions associated with advanced age and terminal conditions—depletions rooted in frailty, disability, illness, and a wide variety of social losses such as the death of significant others, the inability to work, and a drop in income. Each of these, in combination with the others, can have devastating effects on older clients. Mourning or depression over the depletion of inner and outer resources, and anxiety and fear over diminished ability to control aspects of one's environment, are ever present.

The *auxiliary role* is an environmental response to the depletions, temporary or permanent, experienced by the adult. It is a special relationship encompassing the needs of the older person for caring, hope, and empathy, for effective communication, and for care management. Each is dependent on the other. An older person's care cannot be managed in an emotional vacuum; meaningful and nurturing communications with other persons are essential. Nor will the older person survive if practical needs are overlooked. This reality is borne out in the numerous studies of caregiving which again and again underscore the importance of the emotional aspects of caregiving to both caregiver and care-receiver.

The auxiliary role is not necessarily synonymous with the caregiver role, which also includes concrete forms of assistance such as personal care, shopping, and homemaking. Rather, the auxiliary role differentiates the caregiver role in which the caregiver for an old person can fill both roles totally, or share the auxiliary role with others. Though there are situations where the auxiliary role and concrete caregiving tasks are split, what we see most often is the auxiliary role being filled by a primary caregiver, usually a spouse or daughter, but sometimes by several family members. It speaks to the strong dyadic bond that is often formed between caregiver and care-receiver. The bond, in and of itself, can serve as a replenishment for depletions incurred.

On a very practical level, the person serving in the auxiliary role can act on behalf of the older person, moving in at times of impaired judgment or communication, to represent views or expedite transactions. The long-standing relationship between family members and significant other often stands them in good stead to fill this role because of their familiarity with the older person and his or her lifestyle and desires. Frequently, family members are asked to act on behalf of an incompetent older relative, and they feel comfortable in doing so because of their knowledge of what the older person would desire. Older people themselves select family members as their designated stand-ins for the same reasons.

By the same token, although the auxiliary role most often falls on one or two persons, it may be transferred to a larger collection of significant others such as in the nursing home, where the bonding may have to be an institution, not a person.

However the role is exercised, implicit to it is an awareness of the important balance between dependency and autonomy, and of the importance of timing, of stepping in and then pulling back when assistance is no longer needed. The very act of stepping back, coupled with words of encouragement or a gentle challenge, potentially enables the client.

The auxiliary role is a *flexible* response to the depletions being experienced by the older person. These depletions and their effects can vary even for one person: one day a great deal of support may be required, and even someone to "take over"; on another, the older person may be more able to cope unaided. We all have experienced those times when an older person's hearing impairment or confusion may stand in the way of effective communication; on another day there may be no problem.

Sensitivity to the depletions affecting the older person alerts the person filling the auxiliary role to a variety of associated behaviors. Anxiety and depression can be understood within this context, as can more negative types of difficult behavior. Hoarding, for example, if understood as a symbolic reaction to depletion, may forestall negative responses to the older person that only intensify the undesirable behavior. Stubbornness and uncooperativeness fall into the same category.

The auxiliary role calls for very special attention to adaptive communications, particularly for the mentally or sensorially impaired older person. Caring, hope, and empathy cannot be imparted, and effective planning cannot take place, without communication. Ruling out underlying or correctable medical conditions that may account for dementia or hearing and vision loss is a top priority. Given the presence of a chronic irreversible impairment, however, communication remains a critical issue in building and maintaining a relationship.

Vision impairment alone, in the elderly, rarely should stand in the way of communication. Oral communication can be easily expedited and written communication eschewed unless a reader is available or the older person has access to visual aids. Because vision itself is an aid in picking up such non-verbal cues as facial expressions, lip movements, and body language, we must be as orally explicit as possible with the visually impaired person, identifying ourselves when we enter a room and describing the action taking place.

If the client has impaired hearing, the selection of a site for interviewing where communication is enhanced is critical. The room should be well lighted, there should not be noisy distractions, and the communicator should sit at eye level with the older person to foster oral communication, and speak slowly, using short sentences. Consideration should also be given to utilizing an assistive listening device:

a simple set of headphones and amplifier. Written communication may have to substitute for oral communication.

When the older person is dually impaired, which is not infrequent, the communication difficulties are multiplied, for good hearing often compensates for poor vision, and vice versa. In such situations, and in difficult cases of singular impairment, expert help from rehabilitation agencies should be sought.

Dementia affects the ability to think logically and to translate ideas and feelings into oral communication. Judgment is necessarily affected as well as the ability to communicate orally with others. Often, this failure is mistaken for a total inability to communicate, and the person with dementia is left isolated. Yet persons with dementia *can* communicate on pre-verbal levels, in action if not in word. Often they are incoherent. In the exercise of the auxiliary role, there is much that can be expressed and responded to if we watch for their non-verbal cues, listen to the themes that emerge in their reminiscing, tune into the broader context of their current experiences, and even attempt to translate their efforts to communicate.

I am reminded of the case of the elderly woman in a wheelchair who had recently been admitted to a nursing home and was anxiously awaiting a visit from her daughter from out of town, who was overdue. She wheeled to the front desk, repeatedly asking the receptionist if it was time for her plane to leave. The receptionist, who had been clued in by the social worker about the probable reason for her agitation, explained patiently several times to the older woman that she would not be taking a plane trip, but that her daughter would be arriving soon. These explanations temporarily calmed the woman. After her daughter arrived, the pleased older woman commented to the receptionist that she had never before received such courteous attention from United Airlines.

There are numerous other situations where the person or persons filling the auxiliary role can think for, speak for, and act for an impaired older person, stepping back when the individual's condition does not warrant intervention. Close communication *with* and on behalf of the impaired older person is required at all times through careful observation, listening, and adaptive devices. We know that reminiscence is an important psychological tool for very old people to maintain a sense of self. Its utilization is a critical component of the auxiliary function model.

Maintaining a balance between dependency and personal autonomy becomes an ongoing challenge. The emotional bond that exists or is developed between an older person and significant others filling the auxiliary role can in itself be an impetus to effective and humane planning.

THE FAMILY'S ROLE

Given the critical importance of the auxiliary role for the older person, our attention turns to the family who, if available, most naturally fill it. The extent of their involvement in this capacity as well as in concrete caregiving tasks has important implications for family functioning and for the personal autonomy and well-being of the individuals involved. Unless a balance is sought which respects the integrity of the family as a whole, not only does the older person remain at risk, but the family itself is placed at risk. Although there is still little consensus in the field of gerontology regarding the degree of caring and caregiver burden that can be tolerated by the family, we do know that families do give up and seek nursing home placement or other types of help. We do know that older wives physically and emotionally suffer as a result of the extensive and intensive care of a spouse.

We also know that the family gains satisfaction from the help given to an older relative, including emotional support, care management, and hands-on help. We also know that older people prefer that family members fill the auxiliary role and sometimes concrete caregiving tasks. There is no substitute for the trust and familiarity that may have been built up over years of reciprocal family relationships. This speaks to the family's role in determining the care it will give, and the elder's role in determining the care desired. But families must respond to other priorities in their lives and to the needs of other family members. What they can do or not do is a matter not so much of willingness or responsibility as of what they are *able* to do in the face of other demands or the state of their own health.

Not infrequently, all that family members *can* do is to fill the auxiliary role, recruiting other caregivers to provide personal and housekeeping help to an older relative. Family members may split the functions of the auxiliary role between them: one providing emotional support; another, case management. Most frequently, as noted, however, there is a primary caregiver who, because of the bond established with the older person, is the source of emotional and concrete help. The secondary support and respite that can be given this primary caregiver becomes critical, a fact borne out in research findings.

Not infrequently, family members need help in filling the auxiliary role as well as respite from caregiving chores, in understanding the depleting effects of the older person's condition and the defensive behavior that can ensue, and in communicating with the mentally and sensorially impaired. I am reminded of the situation of the daughter who served as the primary caregiver for her frail mother. The mother, who lived nearby, was growing increasingly weak and had become involved in an inordinate amount of hoarding, which greatly disturbed her daughter. A power struggle ensued between the two of them, which only exacerbated the hoarding on the mother's part. Dynamically, the daughter had overlooked the meaning of the behavior to the mother: namely, that the hoarding served symbolically as a replenishment for the losses suffered and the fear of losing total control over her life. When the daughter, after professional consultation, was able to withdraw her demands and listen instead to her mother's fears, the hoarding abated.

Thus, the role of the family is given shape by the auxiliary-function model. Families need autonomy in determining the help they can give, based on the fullest information we can give them. They also need guidance on the extent of involvement required. The auxiliary role broadens and gives depth to the options available to them beyond the more narrow definition of caregiving. Often they need help in selecting and implementing their chosen options.

THE ROLE OF THE SOCIAL WORKER

I have addressed the importance of the auxiliary role to frail and impaired older people, and to the family's role which often encompasses the auxiliary role. The social worker's role in our model is an overarching one: to ensure not only that concrete care and support are given to the older client, but also that the auxiliary role, including emotional and social support and care management, is filled as well, and if it is, appropriately. Needless to say, in some situations it is a role that the social worker may have to perform, at least temporarily. Although it is a role that falls naturally within the informal system of support, it may be wanting because of the difficulties inherent in relating to impaired, frail older persons, or because there may be no family to fill the role.

The fact that the auxiliary role can be a shared one in the various patterns I have described is a key to the social worker's role, which must be a highly differentiated one, shifting from case to case as determined by the assessment of the client and his or her situation. It speaks to a creative use of self within often severe time-constraints. Thus, in the assessment process, the worker not only evaluates the needs of the client and the social supports available, but also measures the required extent of her own involvement directly with the older person and/or family.

The social worker's role can be very varied, ranging from one to multiple interviews, working only with the family, sharing the auxiliary role with family or others, or filling the auxiliary role totally. This differentiated use of professional self allows for a prioritization of efforts among clients and effective time management. Clinical skills are required to implement the auxiliary role or to help others to fill the role effectively.

A word is in order here about the extent of clinical practice that can take place within such a context. Many of us believe that if we are truly to practice clinically, we must have a great deal of time: one or two hours a week and at least two to six months or more. I dispute this contention; every encounter we have with a client is a clinical one. It is the exercise of skill that determines our effectiveness, not the availability of time. The following examples demonstrate both the differentiated use of self and the use of clinical skills.

An 80-year-old woman was persuaded by her distraught family to seek nursing home placement because of her forgetful and confused behavior, and their concern that she was suffering from dementia and that if she remained in her home she would injure herself. Unable to provide the supervision and care she needed, the family sought application to a nursing home and fortunately were interviewed by a social worker. It was the social worker's role to assess the need for placement, but in a broader sense to understand the crisis that had brought the family to this point, and to determine if the older woman was receiving the type of auxiliary support from the family that has been described.

In this situation it was clear to see that this elderly woman was not managing well on her own. She was confused and unkempt, and had fallen several times. An untrained eye would attribute this situation to old age and probably dementia, and would find the family's anxiety a direct reaction. Attuned to a wide range of problems older people can suffer from, the worker also observed signs of a depression: sleeplessness, poor appetite, agitation, and weepiness. The worker also observed that the family was a caring one and trusted by the older woman, although communication among them now was problematic.

The worker directed the conversation away from the family's fears and concerns about the present situation with simple inquiries to the older person about her recent and past experiences. The worker learned that the mother had been widowed several years ago after a long stable marriage, and since then had deteriorated. Her hypothesis that the woman's condition might be linked to mourning over the death of the husband was confirmed by the repetitious references by the client to her husband. The fact that her depression and continued mourning upset the rest of the family was confirmed by the family's insistence that "mother" should cheer up.

Within a short period the worker had tentatively concluded that this probably was a family still in crisis following the death of the father. In their remaining time together, rather than pursuing the issue of nursing home placement, she engaged the entire family in discussing the death and the need sometimes for protracted mourning. She also informed the family of the possible reasons for the mother's mental condition which might be due to a medical problem.

This particular session ended with the family withdrawing their request for placement, at least for the time being, to see if a more open period of grieving would lead to less family tension and better functioning for the mother. The worker also urged a visit to a geriatrically savvy internist to assess the woman's physical condition, drug regimen, and so forth. The bond the worker established with the client and family in this one session was reinforced and extended through an agreement that they would stay in contact by phone if necessary.

The point to be made here is that, in the short time of one interview, a skilled and knowledgeable social worker "sized up" a situation and postponed an irrevocable course of action. Because they felt "listened to," all members of the family were engaged and working together. More important, the family, by following the worker's lead, learned how to respond more empathically to their mother and how to fill an ongoing auxiliary role better. They also learned case management skills and how to use an internist effectively. This scenario can be replicated in many settings, even at the bedside in an acute care hospital.

You may ask: how can a responsible social worker jump so quickly to conclusions? I answer that on the basis of knowledge of individual and family behavior infused with gerontological content, and by practiced observation and listening we can make tentative hypotheses which future evidence will confirm or correct. Our time may be limited but not our clients'. They can bide their time. Clients can make short-term accommodations that will allow them to think and to work through crisis situations. In a number of cases, this process alone is the *cure*. Frightened older people and families often do not communicate well; being challenged from the start to communicate is a must.

In the case of our 80-year-old woman, a return visit in three months, plus medical evaluation and treatment, resulted in a far more stable situation, but did disclose an early dementia that became more evident as her depression and the family depression abated. When it was determined the following year that nursing home care was really needed, the family moved ahead without conflict and guilt.

This example demonstrates skilled intervention on the part of the social worker that did not require her extended involvement with the older person. It was clear that the family was a caring one and trusted by the older woman, but impeded by confusion over the mother's depression and anxious over her failing abilities. The worker's clarification of the mourning process and its effects on the older client and family, and guidance toward seeking appropriate medical care, strengthened the family's auxiliary role. The worker was able to step back from potentially time-consuming involvement that was really not needed, and at the same time avoid precipitous nursing home placement.

The social worker can also intervene directly for a short period of time in special situations that are particularly difficult for family members. In the case of sensory impairment, the worker may be helpful in those situations where the impairment is not openly admitted by the older person out of denial or a fear of being considered "blind" or "deaf." A family silence on the subject can occur, to everyone's disadvantage. A professional worker may be in a more advantageous position to confront older persons who often are relieved to be able to discuss their condition. The same kind of assistance can be given to families dealing with dementia.

By honing our own expertise, practitioners can serve as useful role models if even for only a brief time.

There are situations which clearly require the social worker's extended involvement. Protective service situations are a case in point. Here, often isolated and ofttimes mentally disturbed older persons live in dangerous circumstances, refusing offers of help including medical assistance. They are frightened and seem paranoid, holding onto whatever vestige of control over their lives they can muster. Skilled intervention of a social worker may be the only hope of helping them, short of legal action.

A case in point is that of an 85-year-old woman, a former truck driver and hardened survivor living alone for the past 20 years since the death of her partner and husband. A niece, with whom she did not have a close bond, occasionally looked in on her, but recently was refused entry as the older woman became increasingly hostile and suspicious. Neighbors became concerned about her safety and health, and professional help was sought. The social worker made three visits to the client's apartment before she was admitted. Each time she left a note under the door indicating her desire to be helpful. She also left a small basket of goodies before a major holiday to further signal her support. When she was finally admitted she stayed for a short time, only suggesting ways that the client might choose to use her services. On the fifth visit she helped the older woman, who was suffering from acute anemia and impaired vision, to decide to see a physician. Medical treatment and corrective lenses were enormously helpful to the client, whose mental symptoms abated as a result of her improved physical condition. She was able to return to her former lifestyle, keeping in touch, usually by a newly installed phone, with the social worker whom the client trusted and turned to for services such as meals-on-wheels. The phone contacts turned out to be very functional, since the client felt more comfortable with intimacy at a distance.

Even in this situation, the worker's skillful intervention did not require lengthy or open-ended visits. She was able to convey to this once feisty older person her respect for her self-determination and need for distance, and her need to be in control of her life. The client knew that if indeed she had to turn certain decisions over to the worker, that it was not permanent. Eventually she was able to transfer some trust to the niece, who used the worker as a model in filling the auxiliary role.

I hope that I have provided a sense of the way our practice with older clients and their families, in very difficult circumstances, can be meaningful and helpful regardless of the constraints placed upon our time and professionalism. Starting with the core problem of disabled frail persons— their personal state of depletion—we move to the replenishments they require from the environment, particularly someone to fill the auxiliary role and to carry out broader caregiving duties. Our task is to see that this role is filled, either stepping in ourselves for a time, or helping those filling the role to be more effective. Our time must be carefully managed and priorities set as determined by the needs and resources of older clients and their families.

Looking to the Future

I have looked at practice issues that are particularly relevant to the types of older persons we serve today. I am convinced these will become much broader in the future as older people themselves change and as society's perception of them changes.

As pointed out earlier, older people are as diverse in their characteristics and problems as younger people. Today's cohorts are very different from young people, however, in their attitudes toward these problems and concerning what to do about them. Today's older people, for the most part, eschew mental health services for such problems as marital difficulties, addiction, personal adjustment, or depression. They are part of a cohort group that views these difficulties as weaknesses and seeking help as shameful. They also suffer from a sort of ageism, attributing most difficulties to aging and therefore assuming that nothing can be done. This attitude is also reinforced by physicians who, failing to cure a condition, likewise also fail to refer or encourage an older person to seek rehabilitation such as low vision care.

My optimism rests on my observations of the future elderly who are young and middle-aged today. They are far more health conscious than their predecessors and far more likely to use mental health and rehabilitation services. They are better educated and less likely to accept physicians' advice unquestioningly. Issues of personal autonomy, not only in relation to long-term care but also in relation to death and dying, will be critical.

Many of tomorrow's older people will be more affluent than today's, and will be seeking a variety of services that social workers can provide, including retirement, marital, sexual, and family counseling. In the future, the able elderly will be as prominent as the disabled poorer elderly. Will our service systems, now so narrowly targeted to long-term care, be able to expand their focus? Will social workers in clinical practice expand the parameters of clients they are interested in serving?

The question facing us is whether we, as a profession, are ready to meet this demand. Is our gerontological knowledge-base firm enough to understand and help with the unique developmental issues and dynamics of late life? Have we closely examined our own attitudes and belief systems so that we can deal with counter-transference issues that are likely to arise?

The future elderly will present other challenges to us. Poverty is very likely to increase for minority elderly and for women in particular. What help are we ready and able to give to the grandmothers of "crack babies" who must rear these children in spite of their own frailty? Are we ready to cope with the ethnic and language diversity presented by growing numbers of minority elderly persons?

As the population of old moves out of the narrow confines of disability concerns, can we as a profession also move? Can we put aside old assumptions and biases separating aging from age-related diseases? Can we look to the potential of our own profession who are "aging out?" Are we willing to confront the difficult ethical issues faced at the end of life? Can we look less at the nuclear family and focus more on the multigenerational family that is with us now and will continue into the future? Unless unforeseen cures come along, the disabled and mentally impaired elderly will be with us. But so will many others. The opportunities for exciting and meaningful work with older persons are very real indeed.

Reference

Silverstone, B. & Burack-Weiss, A. (1983). *Social work practice with the frail elderly and their families: The auxiliary function model.* Springfield, IL: Thomas.

2

Developmental Theories in the Second Half of Life

Lynn M. Tepper

DEVELOPMENTAL ISSUES

THE NATURE OF BIOPSYCHOSOCIAL CHANGES in later adulthood has been scientifically discussed only within the past 30 years. This is due largely to the vast expansion in knowledge about aging and the aged during the past three decades as well as the sharp increase in the number of older persons. It is only since the 1970s that the "interdisciplinary perspective" has been introduced to help understand the interaction of the biological, psychological, social, and cultural processes in the aging individual.

The course of adult development brings with it important events and milestones that signify role changes. These changes are intimately related to the individual's progress through the life cycle because they are significant, sometimes age-related turning points influencing self-concept and psychosocial life. These events and milestones include, but are not limited to, marriage, parenthood, children leaving home, death of parents, menopause, grandparenthood, retirement, death of spouse, great-grandparenthood, and death.

In an effort to explain the processes that influence aging, developmental theorists have created theoretical frameworks and propositions that reflect the results of their research. They have approached their research with questions that, when answered, will explain why certain relationships exist among concepts. Theories are often re-tested, resulting in new questions that often prompt additional research.

Theories can be used as predictors of development and to identify important factors that influence practice.

Developmental theories seek to explain the patterns of change in persons from birth to death. Because adults continue to develop from young adulthood through late old age, understanding the nature of development is the goal of developmental theorists. Some theories take the form of sequential stages; others focus on stability *vs.* change in specific elements of personality; and still others are social/ environmental and focus on role changes. Some developmental theories have evolved out of biographical material and clinical work; others incorporate multi-dimensional influences. Although not every theory that has been developed can be discussed here, several developmental theories will be presented which represent different perspectives in viewing adult development in the second half of life.

THE SECOND HALF OF LIFE

Erik Erikson (1963) was the first developmental theorist to expand previous stage theories to include adulthood and aging issues. His eight stages of development represent a series of eight crucial turning points in the span from birth to death. He viewed each stage as representing an issue offering a unique challenge to the individual. He described these stages as "turning points" which must be negotiated successfully in order to negotiate future stages. Although this stage theory was originally designed to be epigenetic in nature, the issues in earlier stages may well reappear and may need to be renegotiated or modified to meet the individual's needs.

Erikson's Eight Stages of Development

Stage	Life Stage	Issues	Resolved Value
1	Infancy	Trust *vs.* Mistrust	Hope
2	Early Childhood	Autonomy *vs.* Shame and Doubt	Will
3	Pre-School	Initiative *vs.* Guilt	Purpose
4	School Age	Industry *vs.* Inferiority	Competence

5	Adolescence	Identity *vs.* Identity Confusion	Fidelity
6	Young Adulthood	Intimacy *vs.* Isolation	Love
7	Middle Age	Generativity *vs.* Stagnation	Care/Concern
8	Old Age	Integrity *vs.* Despair	Wisdom

Although each stage involves important issues that may influence subsequent stages, the focus here is on the last two stages, which are concerned with middle age and old age.

Erikson's seventh stage, Generativity *vs.* Stagnation (self-absorption), can be and often is the longest of the stages, because it requires that we produce something that will ultimately outlive us, and leave our mark upon the world as proof that we once existed (generativity). The tasks involved in this stage are often met through work achievements or parenthood. The negative resolution of this stage produces a sense of stagnation, or self-absorption. Care and concern are the outcomes of the stage. Since this stage is roughly related to the period of middle age, pressures for occupational achievements and the launching of independent, successful children are ever present. If previous-stage issues have not have been fully resolved, issues regarding fidelity, love, and competence may reappear. Perhaps this is why the term "mid-life crisis" has been coined.

Erikson's eighth and final stage, Integrity *vs.* Despair, most likely begins when we become aware of the limited number of years we have left to live, and begin to contemplate the proximity of our own death. The task at hand is to look back upon our life, including our accomplishments and our disappointments, and to realize the meaning of our life as we have lived it, thereby achieving ego-integrity. When one's life is ultimately self-evaluated as meaningless or wasted, with many "sins of omission" (what *ought* to have been done but was not) and "sins of commission" (what *was* done, but should not have been done), a sense of disgust and despair results. The ability to weigh the positive and negative aspects of one's life, to come to terms with how it has been lived, and as a result to feel that it has had some meaningful outcomes is the essence of this stage, and ultimately produces wisdom.

Peck (1968) elaborated upon and expanded Erikson's model for these two last stage, identifying four central issues or subtasks of middle age: (1) Valuing wisdom *vs.* physical powers (i.e., those who have valued body strength and physical beauty become increasingly depressed as these decline; focusing on sustained mental abilities and achievements results in better adaptation); (2) Socializing *vs.* sexualizing in human relationships (i.e., redefining men and women as companions and individuals and placing less emphasis on the sexual element may improve the marital relationship and provide a greater depth of understanding); (3) Emotional flexibility *vs.* emotional impoverishment (i.e., the ability to shift emotional investments so that losses such as parents, friends, and dependent children are replaced by new friends and new emotional ties with children and their families); and (4) Mental flexibility *vs.* mental rigidity (i.e., being flexible in establishing new experiences and new interpretations as opposed to being dominated by past habits which may discourage personal growth).

Peck also elaborated upon Erikson's eighth stage (old age), viewing three issues as relevant: (1) Ego-differentiation *vs.* work-role pre-occupation (i.e., establishing a wide range of pleasurable activities so that retirement or the departure of children from home does not result in feelings of rolelessness); (2) Body transcendence *vs.* body pre-occupation (i.e., valuing social, mental, and creative activities that enable one to go beyond pre-occupation with an aging body); (3) Ego-transcendence *vs.* ego-preoccupation (i.e., leaving a legacy through human relationships and social contributions which represents gratification and remembrance by future generations).

LIFE TRANSITIONS

As adults move through the various role-related transitions of their middle and later years, the issue of continuity *vs.* change with respect to personality emerges. This issue has been formally studied and debated since the 1950s, when the Kansas City Study of Adult Personality was conducted at The University of Chicago. The first of such large-scale studies of adults aged 40 to 80, residing in the community, it contained both cross-sectional and longitudinal information from which dozens of major publications emerged. Among its findings, this study identified three age-related personality changes:

1. A shift in gender role perceptions in the direction of women becoming more accepting of their own aggressive, egocentric impulses, and men more accepting of their own affiliative and nurturing impulses. This increasing similarity of gender behavior as men and women grow older may be due to the decreased importance of parental roles, termed the "parental imperative," after children have matured (Gutmann, 1977).

2. A shift toward increased interiority, beginning in middle age, as a tendency toward increased introspection and self-reflection. This trait becomes more noticeable in later life, when the individual tends to reminisce and review the events, both positive and negative, that occurred during the course of life (Neugarten, Havighurst, & Tobin, 1968).

3. A shift in coping styles, found to be related more to lifestyle than to age factors. Aspects that influence adaptation, such as goal-oriented behavior, coping style, and life-satisfaction, were found to remain relatively consistent over time (Neugarten, Havighurst, & Tobin, 1968). But a shift in ego style from active mastery to passive mastery was also seen, using projective testing. Active mastery involves striving for control, autonomy, and competency, and requires aggressive action on the part of the individual. Passive mastery, in contrast, involves gaining control over one's environment by accommodating others who are perceived to be more powerful; it is seen as gentle, mild-mannered, soft-spoken demeanor, and may be related to the shift in gender role changes over the life course.

Lowenthal and associates (1975) examined four age groups, all of which were in transitional phases of life. These included high school seniors, newly-weds, middle-aged parents, and pre-retirees. An extensive amount of material was gathered, through interviews and personality tests, on issues related to perceptions of change, lifestyle configurations, self-image, views on one's lifestyle, and preoccupation with stress. Certain themes emerged. Family-centeredness was a major characteristic in every group, although it was manifested in various ways: parenthood was a major goal for the two younger groups; older women tended to redirect this child-centered focus to their husbands. There was wide variation over the life course on measures of lifestyle, self-concept, social interaction, values and goals, and emotional experience. Individuals having limited role involvement and few social activities were referred to as simplistic; those who had many roles and were involved in a wide variety of activities were referred to as complex. Notable trends were observed when levels of happiness were compared to their position on the simplistic–complex dimension. Those young adults who were happiest were judged most complex. However, among older adults, the least happy were complex people, perhaps because there were not enough opportunities for socialization, and their chances for self-expression were limited. Persons in late middle age who reported the fewest life transitions and the least amount of stress (the simplistic types) were happiest.

Sex differences also emerged from the population studied. Men tended to move from insecurity and discontent in young adulthood to a high level of energy in the areas of order, control, and productivity in middle age, to a mellow, self-satisfaction in later adulthood. Women moved from dependency and helplessness in younger adulthood to a more aggressive, assertive style in middle and old age. These findings reflect gender-based alternative developmental courses. We cannot help but wonder to what extent these differences were due to socialization and cohort effects, and if the influence of the women's movement has impacted upon the sequence of development.

Bernice Neugarten, a social psychologist, believes that the social environment of a specific age group can change what she refers to as one's *social clock* (1968). This social clock is a quasi-timetable according to which we are expected to accomplish certain developmental tasks such as marriage, career establishment, having children, and retiring. Events and trends specific to each cohort *set* the social clock for that age group.

Together with Datan, Neugarten (1973) suggested that to understand the nature of adult personality development, we must analyze the sociohistorical and personal circumstances in which adult life occurs. They were among the first to suggest that chronological age has little bearing on adult personality. Neugarten (1980) suggested that in recent years the term "act your age" is becoming less and less meaningful. We are all aware of adults, both young and old, who occupy roles that seem out of step with their biological ages. In earlier periods, it was more reasonable to describe the life course as a set of specific, discrete, predictable stages. Most recently, however, chronological age has become far less significant as a predictor of events such as marriage, having a child, beginning or ending college, career peak, retirement, or even death, for that matter!

Many studies have shown introspection and stocktaking to be a developmental trend during middle age. Valliant (1977) concluded that mid-life is a time for reassessing the true meaning of one's adolescence and early adult years. In his 30-year longitudinal study of male students at Harvard, he found mid-life males beginning to be less compulsive and more reflective of the world around them. He saw no validity in the universal phenomenon of a "mid-life crisis" for a majority of middle-aged adults; the changes involved renewed vigor and challenge rather than crisis. Valliant also explored the processes we use to cope with reality over the adult years, and found that the use of defense mechanisms become more complex and integrated. These mechanisms become more mature, with less reliance on the more primitive adaptations such as denial and projection, and greater reliance on the more refined ones such as sublimation and intellectualization.

In a subsequent study, inadequate coping ability was linked to physical disorders. Subjects in the 30-year study who had adjustment problems were much more likely to become seriously ill and die in their middle years than those diagnosed as "well-adjusted." These poorly adjusted persons had a far greater incidence of heart disease, cancer, high blood pressure, back disorders, and suicide (Valliant, 1979). We can conclude from these findings that positive mental health has a definite influence on one's physical health in middle and old age, and may even delay the physical decline that begins in the middle years of life.

Levinson (1978, 1986) believes that the adult life cycle consists of alternating periods of stability and transition. During periods of stability, people formulate their values and priorities; periods of transition are characterized by changes in these values and priorities. Like Erikson, he believes that these periods of transition are necessary for stages to be completed and developmental changes to occur. Unlike Valliant, however, he sees the transition period in mid-life as laden with crises. Levenson (1978) views opposing forces as key to the stresses associated with this stage, identified in his study of middle-class men, as attachment *vs.* separateness (intimate relationships *vs.* introspection), destruction *vs.* creation (the capacity to reject *vs.* the capacity to create new aspects of life), masculinity *vs.* femininity (permitting both masculine and feminine traits to emerge), and youth *vs.* aging (dealing with one's own aging).

Roberts and Newton (1987) tried to relate the stages developed by Levenson to women's adult development, and found that the transitions were similar but that the timing and the issues were different. Levenson found major transitions for men to be at approximately 50 years of age; Roberts and Newton found this to occur as early as age 30. Family issues were found to be more central to transitions for women, but the idea that stability and transition are characteristic of adult development seemed to hold for both females and males.

Adult developmental issues are also reflected in the variations in the relationship between a married couple as their children are born, mature, and develop independent lives as adults. Most family–life-cycle theorists base the characteristics of each stage upon the age of the oldest child in the family. Each stage carries with it a set of developmental tasks to complete, based on personal, emotional, cultural, and biological needs of the family members. Family cycle changes in the second half of life begin in middle age, when parents recognize that the children will be leaving home to establish their own adult lives. This involves re-thinking their roles as parents, balancing supporting the independence of the children with providing gentle guidance. The post-parental phase of the family cycle takes the form of three distinct stages: The period between the time the last child leaves home and the retirement of one or both spouses; the period between retirement and death of one spouse; and the period between death of one spouse and death of the widowed spouse. These last three stages of family development have grown tremendously during the past century because, since families are smaller, the last child leaves home earlier, and life expectancy has increased by 30 years.

Significant role transitions take place during these years, such as adjusting to life without child-rearing responsibilities, adjusting to the "couple relationship" that existed before children were born, responsibility for an aging parent, retirement, and widowhood. Elaboration on these transitions and their implications follows in a subsequent chapter.

SOCIAL THEORIES

Two conflicting social theories about aging emerged in the early 1960s, and both sought to explain how the greatest amount of success and satisfaction can be derived in later life. These theories were called the disengagement theory and the activity theory of aging. Both attempted to describe and predict how a person may respond to old age.

Disengagement theory was developed as a result of the work of Cumming and Henry (1961), and contends that it is normal and inevitable for people as they age to begin to give up specific roles, activities, and interests and slowly to withdraw from participation in society. Society, it was held, mutually disengages the older person because it requires people with new energy and skills. The older person becomes more self-absorbed, reduces emotional ties, and is less interested in worldly affairs. This self-preoccupation was considered beneficial for aging successfully. This theory has been highly criticized by gerontologists, as it supports social myths and stereotypes related to aging and the aged. Some of these are that social withdrawal is inevitable and the elderly welcome it; that high activity results in low morale; that life-satisfaction in old age is associated with fewer roles; and that disengagement is usually mutually welcomed. Disengagement theory continues to be under attack; some of the research generated by the controversy supports disengagement, but most of it does not.

Activity theory, conversely, states that continued social interaction and productivity are essential to a sense of well-being and life-satisfaction in old age. It implies that a comfortable level of social activity is essential for people of all ages. This theory also suggests that it is healthy for older people to continue roles that were held in middle age for as long as possible. The more active an older person is, the more likely it is that he or she will experience a higher level of satisfaction with life. This may be true as a general rule, but it is certainly not a predictor, in and of itself, of life-satisfaction for everyone. A well-known study which was an outgrowth of the Kansas City Study investigated the controversy of engagement *vs.* disengagement (Neugarten, Havighurst, and Tobin, 1968), and found that involvement and activity were more often than not associated with life-satisfaction.

In working with older people, practitioners should consider other factors related to mental health. Previous personality, likes and dislikes, physical and mental health, attitudes toward former and current social and work roles, and identities which have been especially rewarding are factors that are important to assess when designing programs and interventions, and providing services for the older adult. A third theory could logically emerge from the activity and disengagement theories: a "substitution theory." This considers the pros and cons of activity and disengagement, and is based on the assessment factors stated above. It would acknowledge activity and involvement as important for life-satisfaction, but would consider that certain social and work roles are disengaged from because of predetermined rules (such as retirement), or because of chance (such as marriage and parenthood), for economic reasons (such as retirement, insufficient social or private pension income, and recession), or for health factors (such as sensory changes, arthritis, and reduced energy level)—either voluntarily or involuntarily. Substitution theory suggests that individuals, as they age, substitute *new* activities, interests, involvements, and people for those which they have become disengaged. It suggests that a comfortable level of activity be maintained (i.e., not increased or decreased) that will ensure continuity of life-satisfaction and not compromise quality of life.

In working with older persons, one final developmental concept should be noted which influences practically all service delivery systems. Locus of control, a personality characteristic that tends to remain fairly constant through-out the adult life span, is a factor influencing life-satisfaction. The locus (or center) of control is perceived as *internal* if individuals feel that they are in control, and that they are largely responsible for what happens to them. They believe that positive change can occur through their own efforts and actions. They take responsibility for events in their lives because they tend not to believe in luck or fate. Conversely, the locus of control is considered to be *external* if individuals perceive themselves as not having influence on their lives, and ultimately leave all successes and failures up to chance, fate, luck, or the power of others. Persons with an internal locus of control experience more control over the environ-ment, and therefore are more likely to improve conditions that affect them. Adults of all ages, young or old, experience a better quality of life and a higher life-satisfaction when their control is internal. The social environment often feeds back information to us about the sense of control we have over conditions in our lives. Therefore, when the feedback is positive, the development of internal control is more predict-able. In order to establish this internal control, and reinforce

its consequences, older people should be able to make decisions that will directly influence them, experience self-determination in as many aspects of life as possible, and influence
policies that will affect them. Empowerment is a natural
pre-requisite for developing higher life-satisfaction and improving one's quality of life.

Conclusion

This essay has described some of the more common patterns
that emerge in later life, and can serve as points of departure
for considerations in working with older people in specific
situations. This population tends not to want to be dependent on others any more than it must, desiring to preserve
every bit of independence, personal autonomy, and self-
respect. Providing assistance to persons with such attitudes
and values is not easy, but extremely rewarding.

Social workers who work with older people need to recognize the great diversity that exists among this population.
We need to place emphasis on working with the elderly as
individuals, taking into consideration all the concurrent
roles and interactions between them and their families.
Assumptions need to be avoided which relate the psychosocial lives of the elderly to society's stereotypes or our own
biases based on personal experience. Individual differences
among the elderly such as sex, income, health, social class,
and ethnic group membership are also important to consider when interventions are proposed. Acknowledging the
great diversity of lifestyles and preferences will result in
decision making, problem solving, and program planning
that will meet the explicit needs of the elderly individual.

References

Cumming, E., & Henry, W. E. (1961). *Growing old: The process of
disengagement.* New York: Basic Books.

Erikson, E. H. (1963). *Childhood and society* (2nd ed.). New York: Norton.

Gutmann, D. (1977). The cross-cultural perspective: Notes toward a comparative psychology of aging. In J. Birren & K. W. Schaie (Eds.), *Handbook of the psychology of aging* (pp. 302–326). New York: Van Nostrand Reinhold.

Levinson, D. (1978). *The seasons of a man's life.* New York: Knopf.

Levinson, D. (1986). A conception of adult development. *American Psychologist, 41*, 3–13.

Lowenthal, M., Thurner, M., & Chiriboga, D. (1975). *Four stages of life.* San Francisco: Jossey-Bass.

Neugarten, B. L. (1980). Act your age: Must everything be a midlife crisis? In *Annual Editions: Human Development.* Guilford, CT: Dushkin.

Neugarten, B. L., & Datan, N. (1973). Sociological perspectives in the life cycle. In P. Baltes & K. W. Schaie (Eds.), *Lifespan Developmental Psychology* (pp. 53–69). New York: Academic Press.

Neugarten, B. L., Havighurst, R., & Tobin, S. (1968). Personality and patterns of aging. In B. Neugarten (Ed.), *Middle age and aging* (pp. 173–177). Chicago: The University of Chicago Press.

Peck, R. (1968). Psychological development in the second half of life. In B. L. Neugarten (Ed.), *Middle age and aging* (pp. 88–92). Chicago: The University of Chicago Press.

Roberts, P., & Newton, P. (1987). Levinsonian studies of women's adult development. *Psychology and Aging, 2*, 154–163.

Valliant, G. E. (1977). *Adaptation to life.* Boston: Little, Brown.

Valliant, G. E. (1979). Natural history of male psychologic health: Effects of mental health on physical health. *The New England Journal of Medicine, 301*, 1249–1254.

3

Family Relationships in Later Life

Lynn M. Tepper

FAMILIES ARE ALIVE AND WELL, and in reality do not fulfill the prophecy of doom imposed upon them by public opinion. Family relationships can run the gamut from violence to unconditional love, and are capable of being both the greatest source of pain and the greatest opportunity for joy. They have influenced and continue to influence our lives from the time we are infants to the time we reach late old age. The family of the twentieth century is diverse, and can include same sex or opposite sex partners, sons and daughters from previous marriages, single-parent families, great-grandparents, and so forth. When family relationships become distant or dysfunctional, many people create substitute families. Generally, older people are isolated from their families only if they choose to be, or if they are so frail or impaired that they cannot reach out and function as social beings. Studies show that family ties are the norm in later life, and that close bonds tend to persist. But even when bonds are close, times of conflict alternate with times of relative harmony.

HISTORICAL PERSPECTIVES ON THE FAMILY

We cannot fully understand the older person's personal perspective regarding family relationships without acknowledging the importance of some historical considerations. This means acquiring an understanding of family perspectives for the period from approximately 1950 to 1980. The present population of elderly people married and raised their children during the postwar era of relative prosperity. This period was marked by a belief in "family togetherness," as exemplified by the television portrayal of harmonious, seemingly well-adjusted families on programs such as "Father Knows Best" and "Leave It to Beaver." Family problems such as parent–child conflicts, sibling conflicts, divorce, and illegitimacy were thought of as exceptions to the norm.

Many changes in the family have occurred since the 1950s. People are marrying later or deciding not to marry, birth rates have declined dramatically, many more women are in the work force, divorce rates have tripled, single-parent families have increased dramatically, out-of-wedlock births have increased, and homosexual couples have become more public and are making decisions to have or adopt children. As a result of these changes, only about 6% of all families are traditionally "typical," i.e., composed of a bread-winning husband, a full-time housewife, and two children.

Many older people view these changes as detrimental and as an indication that the family is "falling apart." Others have acknowledged and accepted these changes, and even applauded them as positive. Some younger-old individuals have become part of the "me generation" of the 1970s, incorporating intimacy-at-a-distance and fleeing from commitment in their personal and family relationships.

PARENT–CHILD RELATIONSHIPS

Several issues have been identified which greatly influence the relationship between the elderly and their adult children (Silverstone & Hyman, 1976). The first of these issues requires the adult child to "face up to feelings" regarding aging, perhaps frail parents. The realization that there is a need to provide assistance to aging parents should draw attention to the question of *why* help is given. The identification of constraints and barriers that may make caregiving difficult needs to be discussed openly. The fact that feelings are rarely consistent needs to be acknowledged. Positive feelings such as love, compassion, respect, and tenderness are often experienced along with some negative feelings such as indifference, fear, anxiety, anger, hostility, contempt, and shame. The combination of these opposing feelings can lead adult children to behaviors such as denial and withdrawal, which can be counterproductive, and can influence both quality and quantity of time spent with parents.

The second issue requires the adult child to accept his or her parents' old age. The often-hidden emotion of anger can surface and present additional conflict for the adult child. This issue is closely related to the third issue: namely, that the adult child accept his or her own aging. The acceptance of our own mortality and our feelings about old people certainly influence our attitudes about our own aging. Those who accept mortality, feel positive about older people, and possess positive attitudes toward aging are more likely to be able to reach out to their elderly parents. The frailty and eventual death of parents represent to the individual a symbolic loss of shelter and protection, even when shelter and protection are no longer necessary. The fourth issue requires the adult child to acknowledge whether or not they like his or her aging parent. This is closely related to feelings that go beyond social expectations of "honoring thy father and thy mother" and general expectations of "duty." The fifth issue requires the adult child to accept a different role. This new role often results in a dependency relationship, the acknowledgment of weakness, loss of power, and loss of the parents' "parental role." The feelings produced by this role change include resentment, anger, fear, and sadness. The sixth issue is guilt. The potentially overwhelming feeling of guilt resulting from all the above issues can lead to lowered self-esteem and even a subconscious wish for punishment. Unresolved or unacknowledged feelings can provide a variety of behaviors that are often counterproductive in the relationship between adult children and their aging parents. The following represent some of these behaviors: withdrawal, over-solicitousness, domination, fault-finding, denial, outmoded role-playing, protracted adolescent rebellion, blind over-involvement, and scapegoating (Silverstone & Hyman, 1976).

A partial answer to the challenges raised by some of these

issues and the resultant feelings and behaviors these issues elicit is the communication of feelings. Families often talk *at* each other instead of *with* each other. This may have always been their family system's style. Adult children need to communicate feelings to each other as well as to their parents; older people also need to open communication lines to their adult children. There is often a need for families to have "forums" where all concerned are present and feelings can be expressed without fear of the consequences. Short-term family counseling can facilitate this goal.

Adult children's behavior and attitudes are often shaped by their parents' behavior. Silverstone and Hyman (1976) have identified specific behaviors that greatly influence the response of adult children. Parents may employ manipulation to get what they want. Denial of infirmities involves pretending that no problems exist and that all is well (this is often used to prevent placement into a long–term-care facility). The exaggeration of infirmities involves the exploitation of their age (this is often done as a play for sympathy or a demand for attention, and a request for help). Self-belittlement involves putting themselves down for the purpose of receiving positive and supportive feedback. Money-related behaviors are often used to control family members, especially in families where money is equated with love and where withholding money is equated with loss of love. Unfortunately, the family may react to these behaviors by withdrawal or extreme stress responses. But understanding that these behaviors are often representative of a cry for attention and assistance may mobilize the family into action on behalf of the older family member. On the other hand, it has been the experience of the author that occasionally it can be the adult child who is responsible for some of the behavior and attitudes of the older person. Presumably well-meaning family members often consider the older person incapable of dealing with decisions concerning his or her life, and this attitude can lead to forced dependence and a self-fulfilling prophecy of helplessness.

GRANDPARENTING

The role of grandparent is an exciting period of time for most adults, as it represents a new challenge with new opportunities. Several themes emerge when the meaning of grandparenting and the behaviors involved are analyzed. First, a wide variety of individual styles of grandparenting exist. These are closely related to and influenced by such factors as the gender, age, ethnic background, personality, and financial status of the grandparent. Bengtson and Robertson (1985) have identified a variety of symbolic functions fulfilled by grandparents. Grandparents provide stability, are considered to be an emergency resource, often negotiate between generations, and are useful for constructing the family biography. A study of middle-class grandparents in their 50s and 60s revealed that a majority felt comfort, satisfaction, and pleasure with their grandparent role (Neugarten & Weinstein, 1964); but approximately one-third associated it with discomfort and disappointment. Research showed that styles and satisfactions of grandparenthood varied considerably among subjects. Some described grandparenthood as a sense of "biological renewal," some as "biological continuity," some as "emotional self-fulfillment," and others as "a resource person." Many described grandparenting as providing them with the ability to achieve something through their grandchildren which they were unable to do with their children. Others described their role as "remote," and there was not sufficient time to fulfill this role.

Neugarten and Weinstein (1964) have identified five styles of grandparenting, three of which are traditional and two represent more contemporary roles. Traditional roles were labeled "formal": those who left the parenting to the parents, but liked to offer special favors to the grandchild; the "surrogate parent," usually the grandmother, who assumes parent-like responsibilities for the child (at the request of the parent); the "reservoir of family of wisdom," usually the grandfather, who maintains his authority and sees himself as provider of special skills or wisdom. Two more contemporary roles have emerged that tend to be characteristic of younger grandparents. They include the "fun-seeker," who tends to ignore authority issues and often joins the child in fun activities; and the "distant figure," who has only brief and fleeting contact with the grandchild, and is present only at special occasions.

Approximately half of all marriages end in divorce; therefore, there are many older people with divorced children. This can strongly affect their relationship with grandchildren, as visitation rights can be non-existent. This is especially true when the divorced child happens to be a son, as mothers get custody in 90% of divorce settlements. However, both sons- and daughters-in-law have the potential to sever ties with their former in-laws, causing a great deal of emotional pain and anger. Several states have enacted grandparent-rights statutes whereby grandparents can petition for visitation. On the positive side, however, grandparents can indeed fill an emotional void created in the lives of children of divorced or separated parents. They can provide consistency, continuity, and a sense of security to their grandchildren.

Because increasing numbers of people are living into very old age, there is a rapidly rising number of great-grandparents. Most of these are women who married at a relatively young age and had children and grandchildren who did the same. Depending on the age of the great-grandparent, great-grandparenthood can bring either intense satisfaction or great frustration. Often great-grandparents experience a greater amount of disability and related health problems. Being a great-grandparent can provide an individual with a great sense of personal achievement and family renewal, reaffirming personal generativity and the continuance of their family lines. Knowing that their family will live beyond their own lifetime can be a source of comfort that may help older people face death. The sense that one has lived long enough to produce a fourth generation is a source of status to many older people and a mark of distinction.

NON-GRANDPARENTING

Non-grandparenting has become an alternative to traditional grandparent expectations for many older adults. A
growing number of adults are deciding not to marry, and
many married people are deciding not to have children, due
to both dual-career lifestyles and personal choice. Some
have decided to have children later, possibly as late as their
40s. This may be a source of disappointment for those older
people expecting and looking forward to grandparenthood.
Feelings of deprivation, betrayal, confusion, disappointment,
and even anger at their children's life-choice decisions can
become a source of stress. Dealing with these strong emotions without having them negatively influence the quality
of their relationships with their children can be difficult to
manage.

MARRIAGE

Marriages of forty or more years have become much more
common among the current cohort of older people. Because
of the lower life expectancy of preceding generations, very
few marriages continued with both partners alive (and well)
into their 70s and 80s.

Extensive research has been conducted on marital satisfaction, but not much data have been collected on long-term
marriages. Overall marital satisfaction has been measured
highest at the beginning of marriage, falls gradually until
the children leave home, and rises again in later life (Berry
& Williams, 1987). Lee (1988) has reported that marital
satisfaction tends to be fairly high in older couples. This
satisfaction seems to be positively related more to the degree
of interaction with friends, and unrelated to the amount of
past or present sexual interest or sexual activity. Gilford
(1984) has found that marital satisfaction among older couples increases shortly after retirement, but decreases as
health problems and age rise. Critical variables that are
related to marital problems *vs.* marital satisfactions in later

life include, but are not limited to, discrepant rates of aging and health status, narcissism, fear of death, and the older couple's relationship to children and grandchildren.

Older couples in long-term marriages are less likely to divorce due to disagreements concerning relatively minor issues than are younger couples. They may have different criteria for marital satisfaction, which also may contribute to the low divorce rate among this population. Many have witnessed divorce among their children and grandchildren, and this has brought most of them great stress. Some older couples may use this experience to re-evaluate their own marriages, and even to seek divorce because of the increased social acceptance of this decision. Caregiving to a sick spouse is an additional source of stress, and often results in the healthy spouse's being torn between the desire to provide care and the need to have a life, with activities and friends outside this role.

Many of the long-term marriages we see today are the result of stable relationships characterized by intimacy and close friendship. Some may become stressful and even dysfunctional, however, as a result of shifts in roles for each partner. Many of the 40-or-more–year marriages we see today are experiencing a relatively new phenomenon: retirement. Pre-retirement years saw couples busy with child-rearing, with work, and with a strong desire to spend more time together. If the retirement years are not well planned in advance, the couple may find that they are on a prolonged "vacation," with limitless amounts of time together. Working couples now find themselves at home for most of their day; women who were homemakers with set routines now have their husbands "underfoot" all day, as they continue many of their established household routines. Some women may resent their husband's newfound life of leisure, disturbed by the fact that their work continues as usual, without assistance or cooperation from their spouse.

If both partners do not share interests and hobbies, and/or have their own interests apart from each other, the possibility of friction exists. Financial strains may occur if their lifestyle must be altered due to less discretionary money available to spend. Since the average couple will spend as many as 20 years or more in retirement, lack of advance preparation can bring about conflict, anger, depression, and apathy. Even with advance preparation, some couples have difficulty in their long-term marriages. Many of these couples had a marital style of quarreling, and continue their battles into later life. Some have had periodic separations or thoughts of divorce, but have remained together because of their reliance and dependence on each other, as well as their history of shared experiences. Generally, however, strong bonds have been formed, and beneath the anger and quarreling is a close attachment.

SEXUALITY

Sexuality in later life has been studied since 1966, beginning with the early work of Masters and Johnson. Recent studies have reconfirmed the findings of early studies that sexual capacity continues into the 70s and 80s for healthy couples. A 6-year study of people between 46 and 70 years of age revealed that sexuality remained important for a majority of the respondents, although nearly all reported a decline in their sexual interest and activity. Women attributed the closure of their sexual relationships to their husbands (caused by spouse's death, divorce, illness, or inability to perform sexually); men who felt responsible for ceasing sexual relations attributed it to inability to perform, loss of interest in sex, or illness. The most significant factor contributing to present sexual activity was past enjoyment of sexuality. Sexual activity generally remained relatively stable among those couples who enjoyed sexual relations in their younger years. But if it did cease, it was due predominantly to changes in health rather than other factors (Pfeiffer & Davis, 1974; George & Weiler, 1981).

Sexual dysfunction in older males is not necessarily caused by age. Masters and Johnson (1970) found six reasons for this phenomenon: (1) monotony of a repetitive sexual relationship; (2) preoccupation with career or economic situations; (3) mental or physical fatigue; (4) overindulgence in food or alcohol; (5) physical or mental infirmities of either the individual or his partner; and (6) fear of performance associated with or resulting from any of the other categories. Other possible causes of dysfunction include surgeries (such as prostate), side effects of medicine, and depressive episodes. Fears concerning the effects of sexual exertion on the heart is another concern, often unfounded. Some changes in sexual function are medically based or are the result of lack of information about a condition or treatment side effects (iatrogenicity). When a patient is not informed of possible side effects of medication, is not prepared for a prostatectomy, or is told to "take it easy" without further explanation, the result can be sexual problems with concomitant emotional distress. Health care professionals should be aware of the need to discuss these concerns (Thienhaus, 1988).

Recent studies surveying sexual attitudes and behaviors of the elderly have found a consistently high degree of sexual interest and activity, given the availability of a partner. Among some of the respondents, sex was found to be increasingly satisfying as they grew older (Starr & Weiner, 1981). Capacity for sexual intercourse represents only one of many aspects of a successful relationship. The quality of the emotional interaction between partners is perhaps most important.

Intervention strategies for sexual concerns include a medical evaluation which can rule out physical causes of sexual changes, medical treatment if necessary, marital counseling, group or individual counseling, and support groups for those with physical conditions that impact upon sexual attitude or ability (Butler, Lewis, & Sunderland, 1991).

WIDOWHOOD

Widowhood is a major family life transition that requires different levels and kinds of adjustments. It has the potential of causing great distress and forces the individual to cope with the absolute loss of a long-term or lifelong partner, to adapt to life as a single person, and to take on new responsibilities and activities. Living arrangements may be altered. A joint household, characteristically dual in decision making and responsibilities, now becomes a single one. Options include deciding to live alone, moving in with an adult child, other relative, or single friend; having them move into the now single household; or moving into a residence for older people, thereby increasing the social network and reducing the increased responsibilities (such as cooking, shopping, and cleaning). Whatever the choice, the transition is both difficult and complex and requires a great deal of adaptation during the months or years which follow.

The vast majority of aged women are widows, outnumbering widowers by a 5 to 1 ratio. Reasons for this include women's longer life span, the likelihood that women marry older men, and the higher remarriage rate of men. As a result, most of the research on widowhood reflects the widow's rather than the widower's experience. Research on widowers indicates that their major concerns are with unfamiliar domestic and self-maintenance tasks. However, they are more likely to belong to social organizations, to have friends, to drive a car, and to have income higher than their female counterparts (Crandall, 1985).

Lopata (1973a) has found three general patterns of adaptation to widowhood for women. The "self-initiating woman" continued relationships with her children, developed relationships that provided personal intimacy, created a lifestyle that suited her needs and potential, and, in general, adapted to match the resources available to further her own needs and goals. A second pattern was the "ethnic woman," living in an ethnic community, who did not experience much change, was involved in relationships with relatives, friends, and neighbors, and generally lived out her life as she was socialized to do. The third group, "social isolates," never had been highly involved in social relationships. They were unable to maintain their few previous relationships because friends had moved away, died, or excluded them because of their new status, and these social contacts were not replaced. They also had less money, which influenced their ability to re-socialize. More contemporary research on widowhood has shown that there is an increased proportion of "self-initiating women," who develop a new social life with friends, especially if they live in an area with other widows. Higher rates of social involvement outside the home than their married counterparts have also been observed. However, health problems, loneliness, and financial strains may be major sources of stress for older widows.

FAMILY CAREGIVING

When we talk about "long-term care" of the elderly, we tend to neglect to consider this country's primary long–term-care resource: the family. Just as myths about aging exist in our society, so do myths about the relationships between generations. The belief that families abandon their elderly is false and unfair to the middle generation. Statistics sometimes imply false information. For example, we know that in 1950, 30% of the aged lived with an adult child; in 1989, 15% of this population lived with adult children. The assumption is that caregiving roles are being relinquished by adult children, but, in point of fact, the older population is healthier and more independent than previous cohorts, and may be living with formal assistance in the increasing number of community-based housing facilities for older people.

Middle-aged children still assume a considerable amount of caregiving functions. Issues related to caregiving are reflected in some of the needs expressed by this middle generation. A primary issue is that of "role strains." Who gets their primary allegiance: their family of orientation (their parents) or their family of procreation (their spouse and children)? Providing care to a parent without denying attention to one's spouse and children is difficult to achieve. Role strain also involves dealing with what is sometimes referred to as the "bereavement overload" of their elderly parents, that devastating sense of grief associated with repeated multiple and irreparable losses.

There are three stressful situations the author has observed over the years which are believed to be the most
difficult for caregivers: (1) Bringing a parent into their home.
This requires substantial readjustment of the host couple's
routine and should include the following considerations. Can
you talk with your parent on a variety of subjects without
becoming embarrassed or angry? Does your spouse get along
with your parent? Has your parent asked to live with you?
Would your parent have some privacy in your home? Could
your parent adjust to your way of life? Could your parent
maintain present friendships while living in your home?
Could your parent let you be the boss in your own home?
Could your parent adapt to your way of cooking? Could he
or she do simple chores around the house? Could you avoid
overprotecting your parent? Could your parent avoid overprotecting you? Could your present income include an additional household member? Could you take part in eventual
personal care needs of your parent? This decision should not
be made without considering other possibilities, such as
living with several adult children alternatively, living with
the parent's sibling, cousin, niece, etc., or relocating to an
environment suited specifically to the physical, social, and
emotional needs of the older person. (2) The decision to
place a severely incapacitated parent into a nursing home.
The obviously high degree of guilt involved in this decision
produces a great deal of stress for adult children. At this
point they should consider researching the alternatives to
institutional care, such as home health care services, congre-
gate-care adult homes, respite care, day care, community
based congregate-meal programs, geriatric mental health
programs, legal services, visiting nurse services, chore services, and meals-on-wheels programs. A thorough knowledge
of available community services in the long–term-care system may provide viable alternatives to institutional placement. (3) The crisis of contending with a mentally ill, acting-
out, violent parent. Disorientation, memory loss, confusion,
insomnia, and incontinence seem to wreak havoc on the
emotional life of the caregiver. The task at hand is often that
of accepting the fact that this is no longer the parent that

once existed, as there eventually may be no trace of the personality that previously existed. A multi-dimensional diagnosis of disturbing behavior is often necessary considering such factors as the onset of symptoms, changes in family health, family expectations, physical condition, recent losses, side effects of medication, stress, the use of alcohol or drugs, and change in family structure, as these may be indicative of reversible conditions that are responsive to treatment. A team of health care specialists consisting of an internist, psychiatrist, audiologist, social worker, psychologist, neurologist, and radiologist may be necessary to assist in diagnosing these conditions.

DEMENTIA AND THE FAMILY

When reversible conditions are ruled out, and senile dementia becomes the primary diagnosis, the family often finds it difficult to mobilize their forces for the purpose of caregiving. Alzheimer's disease is the most common dementing illness in later life. Two issues are central and need to be explored: (1) How can a family cope with the frustrating, embarrassing, and often disruptive behavior of a person with Alzheimer's disease? and (2) How can the caregiver find ways to ease the stress and help the loved one? The author has observed that the amount of "burden" family members experience caring for an Alzheimer's patient is related to the support they receive from other family members and friends. In many cases, the primary caregiver benefits from individual or group counseling at first. But without involvement of other family members, in the form of more support to the primary caregiver, individual counseling is often not the answer.

Regular family meetings that address the tensions and imbalances in the family system created by the patient's disabilities can be a helpful intervention. As impairments increase, there is additional pressure on others in the family to take over tasks. These tasks are not only instrumental like managing money or cooking, but also affective, like empa-

thetic contact or being a confidante. Families benefit greatly
from meeting regularly, either with or without the services
of a therapist. Family members need to assess the changes
taking place in the family because of responsibilities of the
primary caregiver, and to identify ways of compensating
which can keep the family functioning as a cohesive unit.

Primary care functions have usually been divided along
sex lines, with women bearing most of the hands-on responsibilities, and men providing most of the emotional and/or
financial support. With the current change in family structure as a result of the increasing numbers of women in the
workforce, this may change. More formal caregiving may be
done by hired individuals or institutional placement.

The question often arises: Who will do the caregiving?
Most often it is the spouse. A myth persists that we as a
society toss our relatives into nursing homes. On the contrary. Only a minority of mentally compromised or physically frail elderly are placed into institutions; a majority are
taken care of at home. But when families do elect to care for
a loved one at home, there are a number of critical issues
that should be addressed by the family caregivers: (1) When
the problems caused by the dementia are discussed, does
the family tend to get off the subject? (2) Are some family
members' opinions given more credence than others? (3)
What was the role that the patient played in the family
system before the illness? (4) What is the caregiver's role in
this system? (5) Is the caregiver powerful or viewed as
inadequate by other family members? (6) Are there long-
standing family problems or conflicts that impact on caregiving?

Social issues must also be addressed by families. The most
common concerns include reports that friends have stopped
calling; feeling cut off from the community; feeling isolated
from the world; feeling conflicted about needs to establish
relationships, perhaps intimate relationships; wondering
how to deal with these decisions; concern about the proba-
bility of also being afflicted with Alzheimer's disease; and
wondering who the true victim of the disease is . . . the
patient or themselves.

Support groups have increased in number, and have been found to be highly effective for reducing caregiver stress. They are now available in a majority of communities, and offer many benefits, especially in that they allow caregivers to share information with one another and to assist members to better understand their own experiences. Support groups ideally should be offered together with a multi-faceted program, as some people will do better with one-to-one counseling, and others with a combination of both support groups and one-to-one counseling. Stress-management programs which assist caregivers in restructuring or modifying their lifestyles to promote stress-reduction activities are often offered in the community by adult education programs, courses in local colleges, and community counseling or community health centers (Tepper, 1993a).

COUNSELING OLDER PERSONS AND THEIR FAMILIES

It is clear that each role transition, with or without its concomitant sense of loss, can become a challenge for older persons. As in earlier stages, adaptation to new conditions and situations often bring about a need for support. The older person very often has fewer informal supports such as relatives and friends than younger adults have. Even when family members are abundant, they might not realize that changing circumstances may necessitate intervention. At times, the importance of looking to families to assist with some of the problems related to aging is overlooked.

Social workers, psychologists, nurses, administrators, physicians, physical therapists, occupational therapists, the clergy, lawyers, recreation workers, and planners of programs for older persons all share the goal of improving the quality of life for their clients and patients, and often become involved in the lives of both individuals and their families. Solving problems related to daily living is a goal for many who provide services to the elderly. As with younger adults, many of the situations requiring counseling are crisis-oriented and situational, and demand relatively quick intervention. Other problems requiring counseling are developmental, and therefore may not require long-term psychotherapy with the goal of fundamental personality change. Some problems will have no appropriate or satisfactory solutions. The emotional pain that almost always accompanies the illness or death of a spouse or loved one, the psychological dislocation associated with retirement, terminal illness, chronic pain, loneliness, social role changes and losses, and financial maintenance problems are prominent in the lives of older persons. Counseling may address concerns that are the direct result of these situational changes. These concerns may present as feelings of depression, inadequacy, poor self-concept, discouragement, paralysis of will, unrealistic expectations, and feelings of alienation.

Much of the research on middle age and old age has supported the notion that personality organization and coping style are major factors in predicting successful adaptation to growing old. Advancing years is generally not the sole reason for maladaptive behavior. Coping styles developed in adolescence and reinforced in earlier adulthood are usually still present in the older person. Consequently, establishing counseling goals can be very challenging and extremely worthwhile. The good news is that there is potential for change that can lead to a greater self-acceptance, the ability to reduce and control anxiety, increased self-esteem, a renewed sense of empowerment, and the ability to come to terms with life as it has been lived.

Herr and Weakland (1979) have identified several restrictions that exist when counseling older people. The lack of time for counseling may be a limitation, especially when a service provider's job may not include time for counseling per se. Another time restriction may be the client's time. Years of psychotherapy may not be feasible when someone is elderly to begin with, and may be in need of more immediate solutions to situational problems. Another limitation may be not having an appropriate place to talk. This may be a problem in settings such as senior centers or on home visits. Finding a location that is private, comfortable, and accessible to the older person can be a challenge. Economic limitations may also be a factor, as a large segment of this population is living on a fixed income, with less access to health insurance other than Medicare or Medicaid. The stigma that many of this generation associate with mental health intervention can also be a limitation. This is changing, however, and the elderly cohort of the 21st century will view counseling and psychotherapy as a more acceptable part of their total health care needs (Tepper, 1993b).

Counseling older families requires special skill, much of which is rooted in family therapy. Herr and Weakland (1989) have recommended the following guidelines for counseling elders in a family context:

1. Set realistic goals. It is important to differentiate between counseling and psychotherapy. Helping to resolve situational problems is the general goal of counseling; treating psychopathology which is often related to earlier experience is the goal of psychotherapy. Counselors very often assist in revising situational problems rather than reforming and restructuring personalities.

2. Encourage reluctant families to share problems. This difficulty in sharing feelings may well explain why the family is having the problem in the first place. It is helpful for the counselor to "reframe" the approach so that it appears that the family will be assisting you if they tell you about their problem.

3. Assist families in defining the problems. Families often have difficulty in defining the problems. This is especially true when the problem is perceived to be caused by the individual, not the family. Families may appear defensive when faced with the idea that family interaction (or lack of interaction) may contribute to problematic behavior. Without clear definition, there are no solutions.

4. Gain full participation of the family. This is usually more easily said than done. Hesitant participants need gentle encouragement. If all family members are not available for counseling, several are usually sufficient in order to communicate the effects of family interaction and to discuss possible resolutions.

5. Deal with family anger. Sometimes feelings of helplessness and frustration can manifest themselves as the family's "attacking" the counselor, perhaps in challenging competence or experience. Honesty and validation of the underlying feelings is the best approach; defensiveness will lead to disaster!

6. Determine what the older person's family has been doing about the problem. Ask what has proven to be successful and unsuccessful, and why. This is often a good place to start brainstorming new approaches.

7. Make sense of the family system. This involves taking the time to step back and digest all that has been learned about how the family operates. It requires examining the related facets of the problem; analyzing the context in which family communication takes place; identifying family roles such as who displays emotions and who gets the last word; deciding who the identified client is; and considering the expression of personal power of each family member, and how this may contribute to alliances within the family unit.

8. Express empathy, but reserve judgment. The expression of approval or disapproval is not necessary to validate how family members feel or what they do.

9. Mobilize the energy of the family. Assisting the family to move forward toward a solution may or may not necessitate further counselor interventions. If the family has difficulty moving forward, the task is to lead the family gently around the obstacles that are holding them back.

Family counseling can also be helpful for families of institutionalized persons. It can help them deal with the feelings, stresses, and pressures they may be experiencing about their older relative. Groups organized for this purpose can also be informational, and can provide members with knowledge about Alzheimer's disease, depression, medication usage, physical changes, the meaning of institutional life, and guidelines for visitation (Weiner, Brok, & Snadowsky, 1987).

CONCLUSION

Developmental issues in later life are inextricably related to and result from family relationships. Older people can best be understood in the context of their families. This chapter has described some of the more common family patterns in later life, demonstrating the complexity of older people's social worlds. Professionals working with older families need to be cognizant of this complexity when assessing situations and planning interventions.

In addition, professionals must recognize the great diversity that exists among elders as well as among family systems. Older people are individuals with long histories of family interaction; they have roles and relationships which have both changed and remained constant. Families are diverse in their expectations and quality of interaction. Differences among older persons, couples, and families, especially with regard to the great diversity of lifestyles and preferences that affect their approach to decision making and problem solving, are important considerations when interventions are proposed.

REFERENCES

Bengtson, V. L., & Robertson, J. F. (Eds.). (1985). *Grandparenthood*. Beverly Hills: Sage Publications.

Berry, R. E., & Williams, F. L. (1987). Assessing the relationship between quality of life and marital and income satisfaction. *Journal of Marriage and the Family, 49*, 107–116.

Burnside, I. M. (1984). *Working with the elderly: Group processes and techniques*. Monterey, CA: Wadsworth.

Butler, R. N., Lewis, M., & Sunderland, T. (1991). *Aging and mental health*. New York: MacMillan.

Crandall, R. (1985). *Gerontology: A behavioral science approach*. Reading, MA: Addison-Wesley.

George, L. K., & Weiler, S. J. (1981). Sexuality in middle and later life: The effects of age-cohort and gender. *Archives of General Psychiatry, 38*, 919–923.

Gilford, R. (1984). Contrasts in marital satisfaction in old age: An exchange theory analysis. *Journal of Gerontology, 39*, 325–333.

Herr, J. J., & J. H. Weakland (1979). *Counseling elders and their families*. New York: Springer.

Lopata, H. Z. (1973a). Support systems of American urban widowhood. *Journal of Gerontological Issues, 44*(3), 113–128. Lopata, H. Z. (1973b). *Widowhood in an American city*. Cambridge, MA: Schenkman.

Lee, A. R. (1988). Kinship and social support of the elderly: The case of the U.S. *Aging and Society, 5*, 19–38.

Masters, W. H. & Johnson, V. E. (1970). *Human sexual inadequacy*. Boston: Little, Brown.

Neugarten, B. L., & Weinstein, K. K. (1964). The changing American grandparent. *Journal of Marriage and the Family, 26*, 299–304.

Pfeiffer, E., & Davis, G. (1974). Determinants of sexual behavior in middle age and old age. In E. Palmore (Ed.), *Normal aging 2: Reports of the Duke longitudinal study, 1970–1973* (pp. 251–252). Durham, NC: Duke University Press.

Silverstone, B., & Hyman, H. K. (1976). *You and your aging parent*. New York: Pantheon.

Starr, B. D., & Weiner, M. B. (1981). *Starr–Weiner report on sex and sexuality in the mature years*. Briarcliff Manor, NY: Stein & Day.

Tepper, L. M. (1993a). A life-style rehabilitation approach to manage the stress of caregiving. In L. Tepper & J. Toner, *Respite care: Programs, problems, and solutions* (pp. 157–165). New York: Charles.

Tepper, L. M. (1993b). Group therapy with the elderly. In J. Toner & L. Tepper (Eds) *Long term care* (pp. 136–147). New York: Charles.

Thienhaus, O. J. (1988). Practical overview of sexual function and advancing age. *Geriatrics, 43*, 63–67.

Weiner, M. B., Brok, A. J., & Snadowsky, A. M. (1987). *Working with the aged: Practical approaches in the institution and in the community* (2nd ed.). Norwalk: Appleton-Century-Crofts.

PART II

Issues in Practice and Service Delivery

4

Cultural Diversity and Practice with Older People

Elaine Congress and Martha V. Johns

INTRODUCTION

THE NUMBER OF PEOPLE over 65 from ethnic groups other than European has increased dramatically within recent decades (Taeuber, 1990). In 1990 the projected population for ethnic older people included 2.6 million Black Americans, 1.1 million Hispanic, and 603,000 from other cultural groups including Asians and Native Americans (U.S. Bureau of Census, 1988). It is estimated that these numbers of ethnic minorities will double within the next 60 years (Taeuber, 1990).

While there has been a growth in social service programs for older people since the passage of the 1965 Older Americans Act, there is considerable evidence that ethnic older people do not utilize these services (Colen, 1983). As the need for social services for ethnic older people continues to increase, it is crucial that social workers examine issues of ethnicity[1] as related to aging and utilize this theoretical perspective to develop, provide, and improve social services for them.

This chapter will explore different theoretical and practice perspectives on aging and ethnicity. Included in this discussion will be early theories on aging such as disengagement and activity theories which did not consider ethnicity an important variable. The theory of the aged as a subculture or minority group which implies that ethnicity is less relevant than age will also be considered. Finally the double jeopardy hypothesis will be examined in the light of the complexity of identifying the impact of ethnicity on the older client and in the context of informal family and social supports. The final section of this chapter will address practice issues for program planners, administrators, and direct service providers who wish to promote accessibility, improve utilization, and provide more effective services for older ethnic clients.

DISENGAGEMENT AND ACTIVITY THEORIES ON AGING

For many years older people were considered a homogenous group; both practitioners and researchers assumed that the ethnic background of older persons did not influence either access to or utilization of social services. In the 1960s and 1970s two social theories on aging were developed and debated to explain the adaptation of older people to aging. Disengagement theory (Cumming & Henry, 1961) proposed that a mutual withdrawal or disengagement occurs in aging which results in a decreased interaction between older persons and others in their social system. This process can occur in terms of the loss of paid vocational roles and of spousal and parental roles. Disengagement is seen as positive for both the individual and society and as an inevitable aspect of aging. Mandatory retirement was frequently viewed as a policy application of disengagement theory. Gerontologists have been critical of this theory because seemingly mutual disengagement often is, in fact, one-sided, as in the case of mandatory retirement (Markides & Mindel, 1987). Also, it has been noted that when older people continue in good health with adequate income, they often choose not to disengage (Havighurst, Neugarten, & Tobin, 1968).

The applicability of this theory on aging as related to ethnic differences was never considered. Would older people from culturally diverse backgrounds be more or less likely to disengage? Would this disengagement be positive or negative for the older person? It might be argued that disengagement would be a less difficult process for culturally diverse older people, since many minority older people are and always have been poor and thus more tenuously connected with long-term vocational roles. Yet with fewer benefits from the Social Security retirement program because of low-income or non-covered employment and with limited economic resources, ethnic older people might find disengagement from economic society more traumatic. Also there is evidence that ethnic older people are more connected with the family than are other older people (Brody, 1985; Stone, Cafferata, & Sandel, 1987), which suggests that an ethnic person after a lifetime of close family connections might be less likely to disengage when older. While ethnic older people may experience a forced disengagement from spousal roles because of their partners' death, they may continue to be very involved in their parental role toward their own children and grandchildren.

Activity theory, another early theory used to explain older people's adaptation to aging, was also not explicitly applied to ethnic older people. According to this model, staying active in roles valued by the dominant society or in compensatory roles is important for the older person's well-being (Havighurst & Albrecht, 1953; Maddox, 1968, 1970; Larson, 1978). Critiques of this theory, however, indicated that involvement in roles that are not valued in our society does not increase the psychological well-being of the older person (Gubrium, 1973). Again, activity theory is not explored in relationship to the ethnicity of the older person. Do older people from a specific ethnic group experience more psychological well-being if they continue to be active in roles they had previously assumed? For example, during the current AIDS epidemic many older Black and Hispanic women have had to continue in parenting roles with orphaned grandchildren. Does this continued activity in the parental role contribute to the psychological well-being of the ethnic older person?

SUBCULTURE THEORY ON AGING

While disengagement and activity theories on aging view older people as a singular group without consideration of ethnicity, the theories of the aged as a subculture or as a minority (Barron, 1953; Rose, 1965) seem more akin to the study of ethnic issues in aging. Age, like race and sex, becomes a criterion of stratification. One does not choose to become older, just as one does not select one's gender or race. Because of their lower status as older people, the aged often encounter discrimination in the larger society. In support of these theories it has been noted that older people share common concerns, and tend to interact more with one another than with younger people. Senior citizen housing, activity centers, and activist groups for older people are cited to prove this theory. Again, the question can be raised if this is true of ethnic older people. Are they more likely to identify with older people from other ethnic groups or with younger family members? Asian and Hispanic older people who do not speak English would be more likely to identify with and associate with their own family members who share the same culture and speak the same language than with other older people of dissimilar culture and language.

A singular focus on the aged as constituting a subculture or minority may lead to avoiding a consideration of ethnicity as related to aging. Aging has been viewed as a leveler in that social problems are seen as affecting all older people in the same way regardless of cultural background. Recent studies on similar decreased alcohol consumption and similar life expectancies for all older people regardless of ethnic background have been used in support of this theory (Gelfand & Barresi, 1987). A belief in age as a leveler, however, may negate the very important consideration of ethnicity and its effects on older people.

DOUBLE/MULTIPLE JEOPARDY THEORY ON AGING

Currently, an important theory on ethnic minority aging is that of double jeopardy. This theory suggests that the older ethnic person is doubly at risk for belonging to two often devalued groups, the elderly and an ethnic minority. To be old and Black is seen as "bearing the additional economic, social, and psychological burden of living in a society in which racial equality remains more a myth than social policy" (Dowd & Benigtson, 1978, p. 427).

Not only do many older clients experience double jeopardy with their status as older people and as belonging to an ethnic minority, but they are further devalued because of their gender and class status (Benigtson, 1979; Foner, 1979: Jeffries & Ransford, 1980). Many older people are poor women from ethnic minority backgrounds; these individuals often must endure multiple statuses of inequality.

In order to fully evaluate the effect of multiple jeopardy, it is important to determine if the disadvantage of minorities as compared to whites is greater in old age than in middle age. Because of the differing life expectancies for men and women, the majority of older people are women. Given gender inequality, what impact does this have on an aged person from an ethnic minority? Most older people are living on very limited incomes, and with retirement income often drops dramatically. Many minority older women have always been poor (Jackson, 1988). Does poverty in old age pose an additional threat especially to women with limited lifetime financial resources given the high cost of needed medical care and increased cost of living?

The best way to evaluate the impact of these variables both individually and collectively would be through a longitudinal study. Since ethnic older people have been studied only recently, there is not much longitudinal research on this question. What research does exist usually consists of studying different ethnic groups at different ages. This must be viewed cautiously as there is a risk that generational changes may be confused with changes related to age (Markides & Mindel, 1987).

Despite the impact of multiple jeopardies and resultant inequality and oppression, there is a lack of evidence to suggest that age and/or ethnicity is related to psychological well-being (Markides, 1983). It has been suggested that many ethnic older people utilize coping structures to help them survive in an environment that is not always supportive (Moore, 1971). The role of the church in the Black community and the reliance on the extended family among Hispanics have been cited as aids in helping these groups survive in a somewhat hostile, exclusionary larger society. These informal social supports may serve to mitigate the negative effects of double jeopardy status which ethnic minorities experience.

INDIVIDUAL DIFFERENCES AMONG ETHNIC OLDER PEOPLE

The double jeopardy hypothesis suggests that being a member of a minority as well as an older person places the individual in two devalued populations and thus creates a double disadvantage. Yet it is important not to consider all older ethnic people one group, but rather to study the impact of aging, cross-culturally, intra-culturally, and individually. Three very different groups of ethnic older people have been identified: (1) native-born Blacks, Hispanics, Asians, and Native American Indians; (2) those who emigrated to the United States when children or young adults; and (3) those who arrived when they were older (Gelfand & Yee, 1991). The following questions were developed to explore the impact of culture on ethnic older clients (Gelfand & Barresi, 1987):

1. What generation is the client? There are great differences between first-, second-, and third-generation minorities. Second- and third-generation minorities are more likely to be assimilated into the dominant culture. Yet there is considerable evidence that the concept of the "melting pot" has been greatly exaggerated and that cultural pluralism describes more accurately and with less bias the phenomenon that actually occurs (Markides & Mindel, 1987).

2. What is the socioeconomic background of the client? There is some evidence that the higher the socioeconomic class of older clients, the less likely they are to identify with their original culture. Since many ethnic older people are poor, are ethnic older people, regardless of the amount of time spent in the United States, more likely to retain their original culture than white older people of European de-

scent? It cannot be assumed, however, that all ethnic older people are poor, or, if they are poor, that they will retain their original culture.

3. Where do ethnic older people reside? If clients live in a community where they are surrounded by others from a similar cultural background, they are more likely to retain their original culture.

4. What language do older ethnic clients speak? Do they speak English, or do they speak the language of their culture? Do they speak both languages? For example, Asian and Hispanic older people who do not speak English are much more likely to identify with their cultural backgrounds.

5. What is the ethnic older people's involvement in traditional ethnic organizations and churches? The ethnic older people who participate in the religious organizations specific to their ethnic background are more likely to retain their cultural identity.

DIFFERENCES AMONG GROUPS OF ETHNIC OLDER PEOPLE

Not only have ethnic minorities had differing individual experiences in this society, but they also have had varied collective experiences that impact differentially on their access to and involvement with services for older people. Some generalizations about collective experiences help to increase the understanding of the ethnic older person within the larger society.

American Blacks have been in this country for many years; many can trace their roots back to the 18th and early 19th centuries when their ancestors entered this country as slaves. The experience of slavery, discrimination, and oppression has clearly contributed to a double jeopardy status for older African Americans (Harel, McKinney, & Williams, 1990). Within recent years many Caribbean Blacks have migrated to this country. Older Caribbean Blacks are often first-generation Americans and frequently are very influenced by the cultural beliefs and values of their native countries. Not only do many Caribbean older people from rural environments experience dislocation living in an urbanized American culture, but also because of undocumented status they may fear the possibility of deportation.

Hispanic older people are often first generation and frequently quite influenced by their original culture. Again there are differences between Puerto Rican older people who are American citizens and freely travel back and forth between the two countries and Hispanics from the Caribbean, Mexico, and Central and South America who may have questionable legal status and fear deportation.

Many Asian older people were not born in America. Often they are very involved in maintaining the traditions of their country of origin. There is some evidence that this ethnic group is particularly likely to be dependent on family supports because they do not speak English (Fujii, 1980).

The residence of ethnic older people has been viewed as significant in assessing cultural assimilation. Traditionally it was believed that ethnic older people tended to depend on the extended family and to live in close proximity to them. This reliance on family and on living in communities with others from similar cultures would suggest that many ethnic older people retain their original cultural values and beliefs.

MODERNIZATION THEORY AND ETHNIC OLDER PEOPLE

Modernization theory proposes that many ethnic minorities have moved from rural environments in their countries of origin to a more urban, industrialized environment in America. This move has been perceived as contributing to a weakening of the extended family and to a decline in the status of older people within their family systems (Quadagno, 1981; Maldonado, 1975; Korte, 1981). Modernization theory would tend to substantiate the double jeopardy hypothesis. Although in the past ethnic older people may have faced discrimination because of their ethnic background, they were less stigmatized within their own culture because of their age. According to modernization theory, urban ethnic older people would experience the double jeopardy status of belonging both to an ethnic minority and to an age group that no longer receives much respect from their families.

Differing language often serves to further isolate the ethnic older people from social services of the larger society. Many Hispanic and Asian first-generation older people speak only the language of the countries from which they came. This factor frequently becomes problematic for ethnic older people who wish to access service in the larger community (Gelfand & Barresi, 1987).

Traditionally, ethnic communities have developed structures that provide support and services to their older people. One example of this has been the role of the Black church in offering financial and emotional help to older Black members (Boyd-Franklin, 1989). Yet there is some concern that the traditional role of the Black church is evolving, as Black families and communities face increasing societal problems and older people are only one group needing help from the Black church. For example, the members of many Black churches may be more concerned about the negative impact of drugs and AIDS on their communities than with the less visible unmet needs of Black older people. This might lead to educational or recreational programs for adolescents rather than to the development of formal and informal support programs for older church members.

It is commonly believed that ethnic older people receive much social support both instrumental and expressive from their families. Yet there may be a tendency to idealize this availability (Cantor, 1979; Mutran, 1985; Rosenthal, 1986). Moreover, the positive effects of these familial supports have been questioned (Robinson, 1983). Our previous belief about social supports for the minority older client may have been too simplistic, as it did not take into account individual diversity within ethnic older groups (Lockery, 1991). It is possible that demographic trends such as an increase in older ethnic populations, the acculturation of ethnic populations, and the current economic recession will have a negative impact on ethnic older clients' use of informal social supports. Families can become a source of stress for

ethnic older people, as younger family members often become assimilated more quickly which can lead to intergenerational conflict over accepted values and behavior. For
example, a Puerto Rican grandmother accustomed to short
monogamous courtship and marriage at an early age may
become very upset when her teenage granddaughter dates
several boys with no intentions of marrying any of them.

PRACTICE IMPLICATIONS: PROGRAM PLANNING AND ADMINISTRATION

As the number of ethnic older people increases, the need to
develop culturally sensitive services for this population becomes even more apparent. We will examine what social
services exist and how the profession can make them more
accessible and relevant to ethnic older people.

For many older ethnic populations, the main arena of
contact with social workers is in the health field. It is an
unfortunate, although well-established, fact that minorities
have a shorter life expectancy than non-Hispanic whites,
and that ethnic older people may have more chronic health
problems (Taeuber, 1990) that necessitate frequent contacts
with the health system. Yet hospitals and outpatient facilities usually subscribe to a medical model of disease and
treatment which may be very foreign to an older person
from a different culture. In training staff and in developing
programs, an important role for the agency administrator is
that of cultural mediator, a role which involves educating a
multi-discipline staff about the impact of culture on clients
(Fandetti & Goldmeier, 1988). For example, social workers
must become aware that Hispanic older people often describe psychological complaints in terms of physical symptoms. Symptoms such as anxiety and depression caused by
situational stress are frequently referred to as *dolor de ca-
beza*, literally, a pain in the head. Also, the administrator of
an agency that services Asians must make staff aware of the
stigma attached to receiving mental health treatment in the
Asian culture. The use of intake forms during an initial

interview that require much personal information must be re-evaluated. Certain ethnic groups may find questions about sexual behavior or problems too intrusive, especially during an early contact. Inter-disciplinary teams can be developed which serve to help other health professionals increase their understanding of the cultural beliefs and practices of ethnic older people.

Because ethnic older clients often do not readily seek out social services, the program planner/administrator must reach out to older people from different cultural backgrounds. Social workers can notify ethnic older people about available social services by advertising in Asian and Hispanic newspapers and by making announcements on foreign language radio and television stations. Informing ethnic older people through the use of established minority networks such as Black churches also serves to acquaint them with needed social services.

The program planner/administrator must be sensitive to the diversity within cultures. It is important not to classify all people as similar, even though they come from the same racial group. For example, African American older people who have lived in this country all their lives may have different cultural beliefs than Haitian older people who are recent immigrants and do not speak English. Because of financial constraints, it may not be possible for the program planner/administrator to develop specific services that reflect exactly the cultural diversity of the population. Yet the macro-provider of services for ethnic older people can strive to incorporate some recognition of diverse cultural beliefs within different ethnic groups in planning for special holiday events. The program planner/administrator, however, must be continually aware of differences in acculturation. For example, a Three Kings party for older Hispanics born in the United States may be doomed to failure since this event which traditionally took place in rural Puerto Rico to honor the three Magi who brought gifts to the Christ child is infrequently celebrated by urban Puerto Ricans raised in this country.

The administrator must guard against accepting as absolute traditional beliefs about older ethnic clients and their reliance on informal family supports. The development of more formal social supports in terms of financial management programs for frail older people and day programs for the Alzheimer-impaired client may have to be provided for ethnic older clients, as families may not be as available as previously assumed to provide needed support services.

If ethnic older people face a double jeopardy because of age as well as ethnicity, the social worker's ethical responsibility of providing needed service to a disadvantaged population is quite evident. Often ethnic older people are disadvantaged in receiving social services because of language and cultural differences. Staff should be hired who are culturally sensitive and who can speak the language of these clients. Ongoing in-service training on cultural sensitivity and education is an essential component in improving services to ethnic older clients. The administrator must ensure that the unmet needs of ethnic older clients receive attention. It has been established that although ethnic older people may be poorer than white non-Hispanic populations, they often receive less benefit from poverty programs for older people (Kamikawa, 1991). This points to the need for administrators in programs that service ethnic older groups to provide case management services to help these individuals secure funds and services appropriate to their needs.

An important role for the administrator to play is that of advocate so that ethnic older clients receive the financial and social services to which they are entitled. The administrator must assume this role not only within the agency, but also in the larger political world to ensure that governmental policy and financial resources are equitably distributed among ethnic older people.

In order to increase professional knowledge about services for older people, the program planner/administrator must be sensitive to and encouraging of research initiatives to study the relationship of ethnicity and aging. Initially, research focused primarily on white middle class older people, and much of our understanding of aging was related to this group. In recent years there has been increased interest in studying aging as related to ethnicity, but usually in terms of comparisons between large ethnic groups and general variables on health and social class (Stanford & Yee, 1991). In the past, one problem in studying ethnicity has been the smaller size of subsamples of ethnic minorities, but since the number of minority older people is increasing, this should no longer be a problem. It is crucial that administrators be receptive to new emerging research on aging and ethnicity to help shape programs designed to service the ethnic older client.

IMPLICATIONS FOR DIRECT PRACTICE WITH ETHNIC OLDER CLIENTS

The practitioner who services ethnic older people must become sensitive to and knowledgeable about cultural differences among older clients because these differences impact on each phase of the treatment process. First, ethnic older people may be reluctant to seek service from a system they may not understand or trust. They may have preferred to depend on family support that has become increasingly unavailable. Often, access to service is made more difficult because of waiting lists or required paperwork that ethnic older clients may not be able to furnish. For example, many times ethnic older clients cannot provide birth certificates because they were born at home and their births not recorded. Clients may be the product of common-law marriages, and they may fear the social worker's judgment about their parentage. Finally, older ethnic clients may be uneasy about discussing personal matters with a stranger on first contact. The direct service worker often faces a dilemma between fulfilling agency requirements for documentation and engaging the client. Yet it is necessary for the social worker to establish rapport with ethnic older clients, before questioning on personal issues can proceed (Boyd-Franklin, 1989).

Connecting with the ethnic older client is a prerequisite to providing meaningful services. The family therapy technique of joining with clients and accommodating to their style (Minuchin, 1974) may be particularly useful in engaging the ethnic older client. For example, Hispanics often interact with others more in terms of the personal relationship than in terms of any formal arrangement. This concept of *personalismo* has been identified as crucial in establishing a relationship with an Hispanic client (Congress, 1990). It is important that the social worker who provides service to the ethnic older client initiate contact with the client by demonstrating personal concern and interest. The social worker who accepts coffee at the ethnic older client's home or looks with interest at pictures of a client's granddaughter's First Communion may be able more readily to engage the client for needed social services.

It is necessary for direct service workers to view the ethnic older client as both similar to and different from other clients they have known. In general, social workers who work with older people must examine their own societal attitudes toward older people. They must guard against bias attitudes toward ethnic older clients and thus avoid perpetuating their double jeopardy status. Sometimes it may be helpful for practitioners to universalize, to see their ethnic older clients as having needs and desires similar to their own grandparents'. On the other hand, the social worker must guard against cultural generalizations. For example, all Black older clients are not the same, and the practitioner must continually examine the effects of years in the United States, economic and educational level, and family supports on their clients.

When one works with ethnic older clients, there may be a greater focus on problems because of the greater financial and health needs of these clients. The practitioner, however, must be constantly aware of client strengths. Focusing on these strengths often helps the social worker to empower ethnic older clients.

The social worker must guard against inappropriate paternalistic behavior toward the ethnic older client. Because older people must necessarily depend on others more as they age, there is the risk that decisions will be made by a social worker in the client's best interest without regard for the client's self-determination. This situation is often compounded when the social worker, often with limited awareness, has incorporated stereotypic societal beliefs about infantilizing Black people. With Hispanic clients, a belief in *respecto* which is often translated into a respect for authority often encourages a worker's paternalistic behavior. Social workers who service ethnic older people must constantly be aware of societal and cultural beliefs that might contribute to inappropriate paternalism and a denial of the ethnic older client's right to self-determination.

In recent years, the need for appropriate mental health services for older people has been stressed. Yet social workers who work to provide these services must be knowledgeable about issues that impact on older clients' access to and continued involvement with mental health services. In general, many older people are reluctant to seek mental health care, and this is even more evident for the ethnic older client (Markides & Mindel, 1987). The social worker who provides mental health services to older people must spend time educating ethnic older clients about the type of help mental health services can provide. Social workers must correct misconceptions that mental health services are only for crazy people or that a person who goes to a mental health program will be sent to an insane asylum. At the same time, social workers must actively provide services that ethnic older clients see as addressing their needs.

The social worker must utilize interventions that are suitable for ethnic older clients both in terms of assessment and in terms of the development of treatment plans. It is necessary that social workers improve their diagnostic assessment skills with ethnic older clients. Social workers who work with older people know that forgetting an appointment may not be related to dementia, but may instead be a symptom of depression related to family, vocational, and financial losses often associated with old age. Those who work with the ethnic older person must also consider as possible causes of depression the losses that have occurred in leaving a familiar country of origin and in growing old in a country in which age is devalued. Many ethnic older people have suffered extreme persecution and oppression in their countries of origin. As refugees, they often come to mental health programs with symptoms of post-traumatic stress disorder that social workers must learn to recognize and treat. On the other hand, case management and crisis intervention services may seem much more relevant than psychodynamic psychotherapy. While the referral of a depressed non–English-speaking recent immigrant for intensive psychotherapy may be clearly inappropriate, a referral to a day program for a older client of a different language and cultural background may also be contraindicated. Therefore, the social worker must be creative in both the development and the provision of service for the ethnic older client. Referring the client to an intergenerational program might help compensate for fading family supports, and the social worker can continue to work individually with the ethnic older client. It is very possible that this client has already experienced many losses. Thus, social workers must be careful not to limit their role to merely providing information and referral services, but must expand it, if this is desired by the ethnic older person, to counseling.

SUMMARY AND CONCLUSIONS

The number of ethnic older people in our society is growing rapidly and there will be an increasing demand for social workers to develop and provide services for this needful population. Although early theories on aging—namely, the disengagement and activity theories—did not focus on ethnicity as related to aging, within the last two decades there has been renewed interest in exploring this relationship. Some have denied the impact of ethnicity on aging by describing aging as the great leveler and pointing to research which suggests that aging is very similar across ethnic groups.

In general, studies of ethnic older people in our society, however, suggest that many older people experience a double jeopardy situation of age as well as ethnicity in terms of perceived stigma and access to social and health services. Ethnicity in older people is a complex concept, and length of time spent in this country and language spoken are seen as related to intra-group cultural differences. Not only are individuals within specific cultural groups different, but there is also much variation between different ethnic populations. Although ethnic older people have been thought to rely primarily on informal social supports, there is some evidence that indicates that this is changing. If there is a decrease in available family supports, this indicates the need for expansion of formal social services for ethnic older people.

Administrators who plan social services for ethnic older people must be aware of their diversity and must train their staff about the implications of this diversity. While it may not be possible to develop services that relate directly to specific cultural backgrounds of clients, the macro social worker must be sensitive to these differences in planning special programs within larger programs. Also, in those situations where there are diminished family supports, the ethnic older client will look more to agencies for social services. The administrator must ensure that agencies hire staff who speak the languages and are sensitive to the culturally diverse clients they service.

Social workers in direct practice need to be aware of how they can better engage ethnic clients. They must strive to eliminate their own societal and personal biases toward ethnic older clients. There should be less emphasis on paperwork and formal procedures during a client's initial contact with a social service agency so that the social worker can "join" with the ethnic older clients in a positive, empowering way. Often, misconceptions about social services and mental health have to be clarified.

Many times older people and especially ethnic older people are inappropriately assessed, and social workers must improve their skills in working with these clients. Finally, social workers need to develop appropriate interventions to better serve ethnic older clients. Social workers should envision their role not only as one of providing information and referral services for ethnic older people, but also as one of offering part of a much needed support system for these clients.

NOTE

1. Throughout this chapter, the word ethnicity is used rather than race or nationality since it is the most general, all-inclusive term and provides the "basic foundation for individual and group identity. It is the unifying force that brings a people together on the basis of race, ancestry, nation and/or religion" (Lum, 1992, p. 61).

REFERENCES

Barron, M. L. (1953). Minority group characteristics of aged in American society. *Journal of Gerontology, 8*, 477–482.

Benigtson, V. (1979). Ethnicity and aging: Problems and issues in current social science inquiry. In D. E. Gelfand & A. J. Kutzik (Eds.), *Ethnicity and aging: Theory, research, and policy* (pp. 9–31). New York: Springer.

Boyd-Franklin, N. (1989). *Black families in therapy: A multi-systems approach.* New York: Guilfor.

Brody, E. H. (1985). Parent care as normative family stress. *The Gerontologist, 25,* 19–29.

Cantor, M. (1979). The informal support system of New York's inner city elderly: Is ethnicity a factor? In D. E. Gelfand & A. J. Kurtzik (Eds.), *Ethnicity and aging: Theory, research, and policy* (pp. 153–174). New York: Springer.

Colen, J. L. (1983). Facilitating service delivery to the minority aged. In R. L. McNeely & J. L. Colen (Eds.), *Aging in minority groups.* Newbury Park, CA: Sage.

Congress, E. (1990). Crisis intervention with Hispanic clients in a urban mental health clinic. In A. Roberts (Ed.), *Crisis intervention handbook: Assessment, treatment, and research* (pp. 221–236). Belmont, CA: Wadsworth.

Cumming, E., & Henry, W. E. (1961). *Growing old: The process of disengagement*. New York: Basic Books.

Dowd, J., & Benigtson, V. (1978). Aging in minority populations: An examination of the double jeopardy hypothesis. *Journal of Gerontology, 33*, 427–436.

Fandetti, D. & Goldmeier, J. (1988). Social workers as culture mediators in health care settings. *Health and Social Work, 13*(3), 171–179.

Foner, A. (1979). Ascribed and achieved bases of stratification. In A. Inkeles (Ed.), *Annual Review of Sociology* (pp. 219–242). Palo Alto, CA: Annual Review.

Fujii, S. (1976). Older Asian Americans: Victims of multiple jeopardy. *Civil Rights Digest, 8*(2), 22–29.

Gelfand, D., & Barresi, C. M. (Eds.). (1987). *Ethnic dimensions of aging*. New York: Springer.

Gelfand, D., & Yee, B. (1991). Trends and forces: Influence of immigration, migration, and acculturation on the fabric of aging in America. *Generations, 15*(4), 7–10.

Gubrium, J. (1973). *The myth of the golden years: A socioenvironmental theory of aging*. Springfield, IL: Thomas.

Harel, Z., McKinney, E, & Williams, M. (Eds.). (1990). *Black aged: Understanding diversity and service needs*. Newbury Park, CA: Sage.

Havighurst, R. & Albrecht, R. (1953). *Older people*. New York: Longmans Green.

Havighurst, R., Neugarten, B., & Tobin, S. (1968). Disengagement and patterns of aging. In B. Neugarten (Ed.), *Middle-age and aging* (pp. 161–172). Chicago: The University of Chicago Press.

Jackson, J. (1988). Growing old in Black America: Research on aging Black populations. In J. Jackson (Ed.), *The Black elderly: Research on physical and psychosocial health* (pp. 3–16). New York: Springer.

Jeffries, V., & Ransford, H. (1980). *Social stratification: A multiple hierarchy approach*. Boston: Allyn & Bacon.

Kamikawa, L. (1991). Public entitlements; Exclusionary beneficence. *Generations, 15*(4), 21–24.

Korte, A. (1981). Theoretical perspectives in mental health and the Mexicano elders. In M. R. Miranda and A. Ruiz (Eds.), *Chicano aging and mental health*. Washington, DC: U.S. Government Printing Office.

Larson, R. (1978). Thirty years of research on subjective well-being of older Americans. *Journal of Gerontology, 33*, 109–125.

Lockery, S. A. (1991). Caregiving among racial and ethnic minority elders: Families and social supports. *Generations*, *15*(4), 58–62.

Lum, D. (1992). *Social work practice and people of color*. Belmont, CA: Wadsworth.

Maddox, G. L. (1968). Persistence of life styles among the elderly: A longitudinal study of patterns of social activity in relation to life satisfaction. In B. Neugarten (Ed.), *Middle-age and aging* (pp. 181–183). Chicago: The University of Chicago Press.

Maddox, G. L. (1970). Themes and issues in sociological theories of human aging. *Human Development*, *13*, 17–27.

Maldonado, D. (1975). The Chicano aged. *Social Work*, *20*, 213–216.

Markides, K. S. (1983). Minority aging. In M. W. Riley, B. B. Hess, and K. Bond (Eds.), *Aging in society: Review of recent literature*. Hillsdale, NJ: Erlbaum.

Markides, K. S., & Mindel, C. H. (1987). *Aging and ethnicity*. Newbury Park, CA: Sage.

Minuchin, S. (1974). *Families and family therapy*. Cambridge: Harvard University Press.

Moore, J. W. (1971). Situational factors affecting minority aging. *The Gerontologist*, *11*, 88–92.

Mutran, E. (1985). Intergenerational family support among Blacks and Whites: Response to culture or to socioeconomic differences. *Journal of Gerontology*, *40*, 382–389.

Quadagno, J. (1981). The Italian American family. In C. H. Mindel & R. W. Habenstein (Eds.), *Ethnic families in America* (2nd ed., pp. 61–85). New York: Elsevier.

Robinson, B. C. (1983). Validation of a caregiver strain index. *Journal of Gerontology*, *38*, 344–348.

Rose, A. M. (1965). The subculture of aging: A framework in social gerontology. In A. M. Rose & W. A. Peterson (Eds.), *Older people in their social world* (pp. 3–16). Philadelphia: Davis.

Rosenthal, C. (1986). Family supports in later life: Does ethnicity make a difference? *The Gerontologist*, *26*, 19–24.

Stanford, E. P., & Yee, D. L. (1991). Gerontology and the relevance of diversity. *Generations*, *15*(4), 11–15.

Stone, R., Cafferata, G. L., & Sangel, J. (1987). Caregivers of the frail elderly: A national profile. *The Gerontologist*, *27*, 616–626.

Taeuber, C. (1990). Diversity: The dramatic reality. In S. A. Bass, E. A. Kutza, & F. M. Torres-Gil (Eds.), *Diversity in aging* (pp. 1–45). Glenview, IL: Scott, Foresman.

U.S. Bureau of Census. (1988). Projection of the population of the United States, by age, sex and race: 1988 to 2080. *Current Population Reports* (Series P-25, No. 1018). Washington, DC: U.S. Government Printing Office.

5

Elder Abuse: Policy and Practice for Social Workers

Patricia Brownell

INTRODUCTION

ABUSE OF OLDER ADULTS (60 years of age and older) by relatives and institutions established to provide care for them is increasingly a subject of concern to social workers, health care professionals, and others in the gerontology field. Greater media attention also reflects the growing public awareness of this social issue. What is meant by elder abuse? Case studies drawn from social work practice provide some examples:

- An elderly couple is caring for a severely retarded adult son who is large and unpredictably violent. He is incapable of understanding the consequences of his behavior. His parents understand that they cannot continue to care for him without putting themselves seriously at risk and want to place him. The government agency that arranges residential placements for retarded adults states he has been turned down by thirty agencies, and, because he is considered difficult to handle, there is no temporary placement available for him.
- An elderly widow is found by a neighbor wandering unkempt and hungry in front of her house. She has no family but possesses sufficient financial resources to meet her needs. The neighbor helps the widow to hire a private live-in home-care worker. Not long afterward, the neighbor notices that the housekeeper's son has moved in, and is removing belongings from the widow's apartment. The widow continues to appear unkempt and underfed. The neighbor calls the police, who visit the widow; however, she

denies that there have been any thefts and insists the housekeeper is her "best friend."

- An elderly woman is brought to the emergency room with a broken arm and multiple bruises. Her elderly husband, a former boxer, says he accidently injured her while helping her into bed. He has been her primary caregiver for several years and appears to be suffering from dementia. She seems disoriented and frightened of him. The couple has been living on Social Security and a small pension, and, though eligible for supplementary public benefits, are not receiving either Medicaid or food stamps. They also live in a drug-infested building and have a utilities disconnect notice.
- An 85-year-old man complains that his son and the son's girlfriend have moved in with him and are harassing him, stealing his money and eating his food. But he refuses to evict them or obtain an order of protection to keep them out of his apartment. He states that his son, a substance abuser, "fought for his country in Vietnam" and his son's girlfriend occasionally fixes meals and shops for him. He only wants them to change their behavior, not to leave him.

These cases illustrate two aspects of elder abuse that are of interest and concern to social work professionals. First, they highlight the emotional and other bonds that often link elder abuse victims to loved ones who are also their abusers. Second, they demonstrate the multiple and diverse needs of the victim and sometimes the abuser, as well as the limited capacity of many older people to negotiate diverse service and entitlement systems.

A *New York Times* editorial entitled "Help for the terrified elderly" (April 2, 1991) suggests that with some specialized training, social workers are uniquely qualified to assist elderly victims of abuse. This could include counseling as well as providing practical assistance with services, assessing risk factors, negotiating the court systems, and coordinating medical care. It is especially fitting that social workers should be identified for this role, as social work has evolved into a multi-dimensional profession encompassing not only clinically oriented practice but expertise in case-managing medical, criminal justice, and social and legal services as well. Why is this especially relevant for elder abuse? Like other forms of domestic violence, elder abuse requires a multifaceted response for effective intervention.

ELDER ABUSE AS A PROTECTIVE SERVICE ISSUE

Traditionally, adult protective services have been seen as a state responsibility. Since the passage of the Social Security Act of 1935, casework services with the goal of protection were carried out under the auspices of state public welfare departments. In addition, local charity organizations provided services to adults on their case loads who were in need of protection, particularly older adult clients (Burr, 1982).

Prior to the 1970s, states were concerned with a narrow definition of Adult Protective Services (APS) that focused on the seriously mentally and physically impaired older adult. With the passage of Title XX of the Social Security Act in 1974, states began to expand the scope of APS to serve adults aged 18 to 21 and over. In addition, state statutes were modified to include impaired adults who were found to be in circumstances or situations indicating neglect, abuse, or exploitation (Burr, 1982). APS programs mandated by state statute and administered at the county level were intended to provide intervention at the point of crisis in the lives of adult community residents who were considered to be endangered and who were unable to protect or care for themselves by reason of impairment. As APS programs expanded, however, advocates, legislators, and others began to express concerns about abridgment of individuals' civil rights as guaranteed by the constitution.

Although serious mental impairment requires that the state intervene to provide protection under the *Parens Patriae* doctrine, imposing protective services on non-consenting adults who may meet the criteria of endangerment but not that of serious mental impairment is another issue. Exploitation or threat of harm by another person is an example of endangerment. However, when an adult is threatened with harm by a relative, such as an adult child or spouse, he or she may be unwilling to accept services or legal interventions intended as protection. In intrafamilial situations like this, conflict may arise between a person's right to self-determination and the community's obligation to provide protection from harm.

ELDER ABUSE AS A DOMESTIC VIOLENCE ISSUE

Elder abuse has only recently come into public awareness as a social policy issue linked to the continuum of domestic violence across the life span, including child and spouse abuse. In 1983, for example, an issue of *Time* (September 5, 1983) featured articles on family violence that included only child abuse, wife-battering, and sexual assault. Now elder abuse even has its own journal: *The Journal of Elder Abuse and Neglect*, first published in 1989. Though elder abuse is a relatively new social concept, it is obviously not a new phenomenon: King Lear, for instance, is an example of elder abuse (Reinharz, 1986). APS statutes, as mentioned above, also demonstrate a relatively long-standing recognition in social welfare policy of the need to protect vulnerable adults from harm by family members.

In the 1970s, some British gerontology journals and geriatricians like Robert Butler made reference to elder abuse as a social phenomenon (Butler, 1975). But in the professional literature Suzanne Steinmetz, a national expert on domestic violence, is generally credited with bringing elder abuse to public attention during a 1978 U.S. House of Representatives hearing on domestic violence. As an expert witness, she cited known cases of older Americans who were abused by family members and caretaker relatives (Anetzberger, 1987).

HISTORY OF CONCERN WITH DOMESTIC VIOLENCE

The public's interest in domestic violence began in the 1960s, as concerns about social justice, awakened by the civil rights movement, came to the fore. The civil rights movement is thought to have also stimulated other movements concerned with social justice, such as the women's movement and children's rights (Filinson, 1989). Initially, attention was focused on child welfare issues, and after a number of congressional hearings, laws were passed on both federal and state levels mandating reporting of child abuse cases to state-run central registries. These reports triggered investigations by child welfare workers, and sanctions were established for abusers. Interest in women's rights also increased during the 1960s, and violence against women, especially wife-battering, became an important social concern. Initially, this was a focus of grass-roots feminist groups. By the end of the 1970s, however, it became so prominent a public issue that government began to respond with funds for shelter services and with legislative changes that prohibited spouse abuse and provided for redress and protection through the courts.

The major distinction—and it is an important one—between child and spouse abuse from a legal perspective is that children are legal dependents while adults have the right to make their own decisions about their private lives. This is true regardless of how questionable these decisions may seem to others, unless the adult is judged to be legally incompetent by a court of law. For this reason, government does not have the legal right to intervene in an abuse situation unless requested to do so by the abused person. As a result, programs and interventions established for battered spouses have been voluntary in nature, and not mandatory as in the case of abused children.

Elder abuse has been described as the domestic violence issue for the 1980s (King, 1984). It also presents special problems for intervention. Older people are adults and have all the legal rights to privacy that younger adults have. However, old age is generally recognized as being correlated with increasing physical and sometimes mental frailty. To the extent that one or both of these conditions exist, an older person may be highly dependent on family members and significant others. As a result, older family members are seen to share some of the characteristics of victims of child abuse, such as dependency on the abuser for obtaining basic necessities like food and assistance with activities of daily living. These characteristics are not necessarily shared by younger adult victims of family abuse (Finkelhor & Pillemer, 1988).

Some researchers argue against making elder abuse a special category of abuse, defined solely by the victims' age (Callahan, 1988). Others, however, justify it as a separate category not only because older people as a group—especially those over 75 years of age—share some of the characteristics, such as physical frailty and need for assistance, that can create vulnerability to abuse (Finkelhor & Pillemer, 1988), but also because elder abuse services are most effective when provided within the existing aging services network.

The growing number of older adults has prompted some in the field of aging to become concerned about elder abuse. We know that currently people 65 years of age and older constitute approximately 12% of the population in the United States. By 2020, when the baby boomers will have reached age 65, it is estimated that this figure could increase to 17%. Even if the percent of abused victims holds steady, the increase in the total aged population could mean many more cases of elder abuse in the future (Fulmer & O'Malley, 1987).

Definitions of Elder Abuse

A major problem with all forms of domestic violence is that of identifying and quantifying it. Steinmetz, Straus, and Gelles (1980) called their classic book on domestic violence *Behind closed doors* because of the very private nature of this problem. For this reason hospitals play an important role in the detection of elder abuse. Once a person has been hospitalized, a physical or psychiatric examination can reveal signs of abuse. The victim may also feel more comfortable about disclosing the abuse in the protected setting of a hospital. Community-based social workers can also be instrumental in identifying abuse through the process of providing counseling or entitlement services.

How a social problem is defined has important implications for both policy and practice. One of the major problems researchers face in studying elder abuse is how to define it. The definitional schema proposed by Rosalie Wolf and Karl Pillemer (1984) is one of the most commonly used. It includes:

Physical abuse: The infliction of physical pain or injury or physical coercion (confinement against one's will). This can also include sexual abuse.

Psychological abuse: The infliction of mental anguish.

Financial abuse: The illegal or improper exploitation and/or use of funds or other resources.

Active neglect: Refusal or failure to fulfill a caregiving obligation, including a conscious or intentional attempt to inflict physical or emotional distress on the elder.

Passive neglect: Refusal or failure to fulfill a caregiving obligation excluding a conscious or intentional attempt to inflict physical or emotional distress on the elder.

How elder abuse is defined also has implications for determining how significant a problem it poses for this society. Pillemer and Finkelhor have found a prevalence rate of 3–4% (Pillemer & Finkelhor, 1989). Testimony from a 1990 U.S. House of Representatives hearing on elder abuse suggested that it is closer to 12%; however, some researchers maintain that only one out of every six victims even comes to the attention of the authorities (U.S. House of Representatives, 1990). Difficulties in quantifying elder abuse as a form of domestic violence result both from the fact that it tends to be hidden and from the variations in the way it is defined. Elder abuse can (and does) occur in both formal caregiving (nursing home and professional home care) and family settings; and both settings are of concern to social work professionals. Elder abuse as a form of domestic violence is more complex an issue to address because the emotional ties an abuse victim may experience with his or her abuser can confound efforts at intervention in ways that institutional abuse by a paid caregiver or employee may not. Though the dependency of an elder in an institutional setting may also complicate intervention efforts, interventions such as removing the abuser who is also a employee are possible in an institutional setting; this is not usually feasible without the victim's cooperation in the home when the abuser is also a family member.

PROFILES OF ELDER ABUSE VICTIMS AND THEIR ABUSERS

There are a number of contradictions in research findings regarding the so-called typical elder abuse victim and abuser. Early studies on elder abuse found the typical abuse victim to be female, frail with both mental and physical infirmities, over the age of 75, and dependent on others for her care (Johnson, 1986). These early studies identified the typical abuser as most likely the daughter experiencing caregiver stress, followed by the son and, finally, the (male) spouse acting in a caregiving role. Family stress appeared to be the most common precipitating factor. This could include both external stress, resulting from financial or marital problems or the pressures of caregiving, and internal stress related to substance abuse or mental illness (Quinn & Tomita, 1986).

These findings may have been an artifact of the way studies were conducted and subjects identified in the early research studies. This profile has been contradicted by more recent studies, including the survey of elderly Boston residents by Pillemer and Finkelhor, who found that elder abuse victims were most likely to experience abuse from their spouses, followed by sons and then daughters (Pillemer & Finkelhor, 1988). These findings are consistent with studies on caregiving, which identify the spouse as the preferred caregiver by both older men and women (Cantor, 1991). Older people who care for spouses have been found to experience considerable strain, especially when the care involves a level of personal care and housekeeping chores that the caretaker spouse is unaccustomed to providing (Cantor, 1986).

Pillemer and Finkelhor's study of older people residing in

Boston focused on physical abuse among a general population of elders in Boston. As noted above, the findings suggested that spouse abuse was more prevalent than abuse by adult children, and that older men and women were equally at risk of being targets of abuse. The Pillemer and Finkelhor study in particular suggests that a significant amount of elder abuse that is physical in nature could be categorized as spouse abuse. This could be precipitated by caregiver stress, in those abuse situations where the caregiving spouse is also the abuser, or it could be part of a long-standing pattern of spouse-battering that began at an earlier point in the relationship.

This is in contrast to a recent study of elder abuse among APS cases in New York State, which found that the most prevalent form of abuse is financial exploitation; the older victim typically is female, and the abuser most frequently is the son (Abelman, 1992). Strictly speaking, these two studies are not comparable because the Boston study did not consider financial abuse as a possible form of abuse experienced by the identified subjects. However, it is interesting to note that Pillemer and Finkelhor, working within a domestic violence framework, looked only at actual or threatened physical abuse, while Abelman—from an APS perspective—included financial abuse and exploitation. This could be suggestive of significant differences between abuse patterns and profiles of older persons on APS case loads, who are likely to be judgment-impaired, and the general population of people over the age of 60. On the other hand, it may also be reflective of a given researcher's perspective on elder abuse: whether it is seen as a form of domestic violence or as an Adult Protective Services issue.

In considerations of abuse by adult children, dependency and impairment on the part of abusers have been identified as more powerful predictors of elder abuse than caretaker stress (Pillemer & Finkelhor, 1989). Dependent adult children are defined as over the age of 21, unable to support or care for themselves, and reliant on older parents for the provision of housing, financial, and other support. Though Pillemer's and other more recent studies are considered more sophisticated methodologically than earlier ones that found frail older people to be most vulnerable to abuse by caretaker daughters (and, to a lesser degree, sons), many of the major factors identified in the earlier literature remain salient. These include dependence in old age, a pattern of family violence, life crises for either the victim or the abuser, environmental factors such as the lack of community support services (Hickey & Douglass, 1981) and societal attitudes such as sexism or ageism (Quinn & Tomita, 1986).

For those older adults who meet the criteria for protective services, state APS programs can provide case management as well as legal and social services. But for older victims of spouse abuse, services are limited. According to Vinton (1992), some limited number of shelter beds are available for older female victims of spouse abuse in Florida, but a lack of appropriate shelter programs and services is responsible for under-utilization by older women. In some localities, most of the shelter beds for battered women are funded through Emergency Assistance to Families (Title 4 of the Social Security Act), a funding stream that precludes access for victims who are not responsible for the care of dependent children. This can create another kind of barrier to needed shelter services for older "battered women."

LIMITATIONS OF RESEARCH EFFORTS TO DATE

Most research on elder abuse to date has been in the form of exploratory or descriptive studies (Hudson, 1986). It is difficult to do controlled studies on this population as it could be unethical to identify cases of elder abuse and then observe them without attempting any intervention to prevent harm to the victim. It is also by definition difficult to study a hidden problem. Some of the later, more sophisticated studies have involved large random studies. An example of this is Pillemer's Boston study.

One important emerging area of research is that of abuse among older members of diverse cultures and races. This is significant because what is defined as abuse can differ according to culturally determined values and behavior patterns (Brown, 1989). In addition, risk factors, etiology of abuse, and effective intervention strategies may differ between the majority and the minority races and cultures in this country. Griffin and Williams (1992), for example, suggest that the history and cultural traditions of black families, differences between black and white informal support systems, societal violence and discrimination toward African-Americans, and differential access and utilization of formal supports all serve to create significant differences in patterns of elder abuse between black and white older Americans. More research on elder abuse from a cultural perspective is needed to inform the further development of effective intervention strategies.

MODELS OF INTERVENTION

To date, several models for intervention have been developed, most notably by Quinn (a nurse who is a court investigator) and Tomita (a social worker), Fulmer and O'Malley, a nurse and a doctor, and Breckman and Adelman, a social worker and a doctor. Quinn and Tomita (1986) stress a community approach, while Fulmer and O'Malley (1987) stress hospital-based assessment and identification.

Breckman and Adelman (1988) have developed a model of intervention that is intended for use in either a hospital or a community setting. Although it differentiates between judgment-impaired and non–judgment-impaired (as well as consenting and non-consenting) abuse victims, the primary focus of the model is on the non–judgment-impaired. This cognitively oriented intervention model utilizes a "staircase" approach that identifies the abuse victim as being at one of three stages of awareness (denial, acknowledgment, and acceptance) and outlines strategies appropriate for each stage. The treatment goal is to assist the victim to acknowledge the abuse and stop focusing on the needs of the abuser in order to take charge of his or her own needs and self-interests.

The model proposed by Fulmer and O'Malley (1987) is intended for use with impaired elderly victims of abuse; it focuses on the care needs of the victim and the extent to which these needs are being met. This model is useful for both judgment-impaired and non–judgment-impaired abuse victims; it may have limited application for the non–judgment-impaired abuse victim who is acting as the caretaker relative for a dependent abuser. This is because the model assumes that the problem for the elder victim is a need for medical care and social supports, something that may not apply to an unimpaired elder abuse victim like the mother of the abusive retarded son in the example provided. As part of this model, the authors have developed an assessment tool, the Elder Assessment Instrument (EAI), which is intended to assess the victim's care needs in relation to the available support system. The authors also include a section on ethical issues in working with abuse victims, such as the right to privacy and confidentiality, and guidelines as to when a more paternalistic approach may be warranted. The notion of negotiated consent is stressed, on the assumption that the victim does not lack the capacity to make informed judgments.

Quinn and Tomita (1986) propose a community-based intervention model that also includes an assessment instrument: Elder Abuse Diagnosis and Intervention (EADI). Although this model is designed to assess the needs of both judgment-impaired and non–judgment-impaired victims, it stresses intervention techniques that can be used by Adult Protective Service workers. In many states, these workers are mandated to provide case management services to impaired and endangered adults, on an involuntary basis if necessary. The authors place considerable emphasis on reporting and on the use of legal and court-based intervention strategies, including guardianships, to prevent further victimization and exploitation. Quinn and Tomita are also sensitive to the issue of burn-out in workers who may be assigned to elderly victims of abuse. The authors' suggestions for addressing this problem include ways in which workers can remain engaged but limit their emotional investment, and strategies they can use to ensure their personal safety when working with victims living in violent households.

INSTITUTIONAL ELDER ABUSE

Of these three intervention models, cited by Wolf as the most comprehensive to date (U.S. House of Representatives, 1989), only that of Fulmer and O'Malley addresses the problem of institutional abuse. This is because their model is medically based and intended for implementation in a hospital setting. Most states have laws mandating reporting of elder abuse in nursing home settings to a state office with oversight responsibilities for residential health care facilities. In New York State, for example, New York State Public Health Law, section 2803-D, requires employees and licensed health professionals in nursing homes to report any instances of patient abuse, mistreatment, or neglect to the New York State Department of Health. Though many states have quality assurance programs for Medicare- and Medicaid-funded home-care programs, procedures for the reporting of abuse by a home attendant or other health care professional in home settings differ by state and locality.

The ability of independent providers or vendors to provide care to adults in their own homes without a license or oversight by state or local regulatory agencies make this a form of institutional care vulnerable to abuse. Though in theory relationships between clients and professional caregivers are not as emotionally intertwined as relationships with family members, in reality significant bonds can form that leave elders vulnerable to exploitation. The example given at the beginning of this chapter of the older woman whose housekeeper's son moves in demonstrates this, and professionals working with older people should remain sensitive to the possibility that strong ties can develop between older people and their paid caregivers.

Although formal home-based care for the elderly can provide opportunities for institutional abuse that is difficult to monitor, home care can also form the basis of a protective care plan in cases of abuse by informal caregivers or non-caregiving relatives. Home-care workers, including aides and nurses, can be valuable in detecting instances of elder abuse (Kinderknecht, 1986). A service plan that includes home care can act as a deterrent to abusers who are family members. Home-care workers can also monitor abusive behavior by family members and alert the police if abusive acts are witnessed. However, in a violent household, a home-care worker could also become the target of abuse. Care should be taken to assess any potential danger to the home-care worker when including home care as part of a protective plan for abuse victims.

A service plan that includes the provision of home care is most appropriate when the informal caregiver is overwhelmed and incapable of providing effective care. Such an example is given at the beginning of the chapter: the older husband suffering from dementia who is attempting to care for his frail and disoriented wife. Situations in which it may be inappropriate to place a home-care worker include those in which the abuser is physically dangerous due to untreated mental illness or substance abuse.

INDICATORS OF ABUSE

The intervention models outlined here include assessment instruments designed to elicit information on possible abuse in the face of the victim's denial that abuse has in fact occurred. The American Association of Retired Persons (AARP) has published materials designed to educate older people and their family members about elder abuse, including how to identify and prevent it (AARP, 1987). The materials are specifically designed to apply to domestic settings, but could be useful in institutional settings as well. Behaviors in older people that could indicate they are victims of abuse include: increased depression, anxiety, withdrawn or timid behavior, hostility, unresponsiveness, confusion, unexplained physical injuries, unexplained impoverishment, longing for death, vague health complaints, obsequiousness, and physician-hopping.

AARP also identifies some signs that caregivers could be exploiting elders, such as giving conflicting stories, excusing failure to provide care, aggressive or defensive behavior, withholding food or medication, shifting blame onto the elder, substance abuse, unexplained sudden affluence, depression or preoccupation or mounting resentment toward the older person. Although these indicators have been identified with a dependent older person and responsible caregiver in mind, they can also apply to situations involving an unimpaired older adult caregiver and a dependent impaired relative who is exploitative and abusive.

Other possible indicators of abuse include environmental conditions such as hazardous conditions in the house or apartment, soiled bedding and furniture, spoiled food and the presence of rotting garbage. The physical appearance of both the older adult and family members can also be clues (Missouri Department of Social Services, 1981). Because elder abuse can take many forms, from neglecting caregiving tasks that a caretaker relative has committed to providing, to financial exploitation, to outright physical abuse, workers who suspect abuse of an elderly client must be alert to a broad range of possible symptoms.

POLICY ISSUES

Federal interest in elder abuse began with the testimony of Steinmetz during a 1978 House of Representatives committee hearing on domestic violence (Rinkle, 1989). Since then, there have been numerous hearings on elder abuse. In spite of this, little in the way of funding for programs has been forthcoming. Although federal legislation aimed specifically at the problem of elder abuse has not been passed, there are several social service programs that offer opportunities for elder abuse services. These include the Older Americans Act, the Family Violence Prevention and Treatment Act and the

Social Services Block Grant (formerly Title XX of the Social Security Act).

Programs evolving from these various funding sources have tended to target different segments of the elder abuse population. Funds appropriated through the Older Americans Act and channeled through state and local offices on aging have been used primarily for services to the mentally intact victim; those from the Social Services Block Grant are channeled through state departments of social service and target mentally impaired older people in need of protection. In an effort to better coordinate services, many area agencies on aging and state and local departments of social service have developed formalized referral linkages with agencies providing protective services to older adults. To date, efforts to integrate service delivery for both groups of older abuse victims have not proven to be particularly successful.

One reason has been the lack of funding for coordinating and triaging service to both judgment-impaired and unimpaired older victims of familial abuse. The consolidation of Title XX funding into the Social Services Block Grant in 1981 has significantly reduced resources for Adult Protective Services, including funds for training of APS workers in elder abuse interventions. Funding for elder abuse services through the Older Americans Act has been increasingly limited through appropriations that are not responsive to inflation. One little-explored funding source that has the potential for providing an uncapped funding stream for case management services to low income victims of elder abuse— regardless of whether the victim is judgment-impaired or not—is Medicaid (Title XIX). Case management was legislated as an optional service reimbursable under Medicaid by the Comprehensive Omnibus Budget Reconciliation Act (COBRA) of 1985. This requires an amendment in the State Medicaid Plan (to identify elder abuse victims as a target population reimbursable under COBRA), approval of this plan by Health and Human Services/Health Care Financing Administration (HCFA), and the targeting of services to those victims of abuse who are Medicaid-eligible. However, it could serve to expand services to some non-impaired older victims of familial abuse who could not otherwise be served effectively by existing programs designed to protect impaired adults.

On the state level, activity has centered in protective services for adults legislation (which all 50 states now have), mandating community-based adult protective services and obligatory reporting laws. Since the 1978 amendments to the Older Americans Act were passed, state and local offices on aging are also mandated to provide some services to elderly crime and abuse victims through local aging networks.

One of the most controversial public policy issues concerning elder abuse is that of mandatory reporting. This is when certain categories of professionals (such as social workers, nurses, and physicians) are required by state law to report elder abuse cases to some designated authority or central state registry, with sanctions to be applied for failure to do so and protection from liability for violating professionally mandated confidentiality. Thus far, 43 states and the District of Columbia have enacted such mandatory reporting laws (U.S. House of Representatives, 1989).

The position of opponents in states that have not adopted mandatory reporting laws is that mandatory reporting is intrusive, ageist, and inappropriate as a response to the problem of elder abuse. It is also thought to reflect a bias toward viewing all older persons who are victims of abuse as judgment-impaired and unable to take full responsibility for making decisions about how to live their lives (Faulkner, 1982). All 50 states already have provisions for addressing abuse of the mentally or physically impaired elder through Adult Protective Services legislation. State laws commonly protect people calling in referrals to APS programs from liability for violating confidentiality in the interest of client safety.

Evaluations of state mandatory reporting systems have been fairly negative (Filinson, 1989). Passage of state laws mandating reporting of elder abuse has generally not been accompanied by additional funding appropriations for services to identified elder abuse victims (Anderson & Theiss, 1989). In addition, because family caregivers of adults are not legally responsible for them in the same way as parents are responsible for the care of their children, the laws could be challenged on constitutional grounds, particularly in instances of alleged neglect (Crystal, 1987).

Even with mandatory reporting, a competent abuse victim cannot be forced to accept services. Because of civil libertarian and other concerns, the right of an non–judgment-impaired adult to make life choices that may seen self-defeating to a social worker or a health care professional is protected by law. The upshot of this is there are no easy answers or magic bullets for elder abuse. The burden often falls on social workers and other health and mental health professionals to identify instances of abuse. After this begins the often slow and frustrating task of empowering an abuse victim to improve the safety and quality of his or her life. Though some service intervention models have been developed, it is up to the individual social worker to determine which strategy and service plan will be most effective for a given client situation.

Addressing elder abuse effectively requires interagency cooperation and collaboration. This is because interventions cut across the boundaries of social service and law enforcement agencies, the court system and district attorneys' offices, hospitals and home-based services, protective services for adults, and the entitlement programs. The case examples given at the beginning of the chapter illustrate the complex service needs of elder abuse victims. It is critical that social workers assist victims to acknowledge that they are being abused and to agree to accept services. It is also essential to the success of any service plan that social service and government agencies, entitlements like Medicaid and public assistance, rehousing and home-care services, family court and drug treatment programs are available to meet the needs of elder abuse victims and their families.

To work successfully with older victims of abuse, practitioners are required to stretch themselves and the resources of their agencies and communities to the utmost. The effort can burnout staff who do not have a good network to draw upon. One way to develop such a network is to form a coalition of agencies that serve the elderly (Bergeron, 1989).

ELDER ABUSE COALITIONS

The New York City Elder Abuse Coalition is one example of a local coalition. New York's coalition was formed by a number of public and private agencies in 1984 to coordinate the work of the voluntary and public sectors around services to abused elders, maximize existing resources, identify gaps in services, and support new service initiatives. Member agencies include major voluntary and public sector social service agencies serving the elderly as well as the New York City Police Department and Borough District Attorneys' offices.

One of the most visible aspects of the Coalition has been its professional development activities. It sponsors an annual conference on elder abuse and three large meetings a year focusing on resources and techniques that are effective in serving elder abuse victims. The Coalition also founded a borough-based case consultation program, in which public and private agency representatives meet to discuss elder abuse cases and to determine how best to coordinate service interventions. As part of this process, it also attempts to identify gaps in services and to support members' efforts to address them.

Most recently, the New York City Coalition reached out to an upstate coalition of elder abuse service providers to form a statewide coalition. One advantage of a statewide coalition is that it can advocate more effectively for legislative changes and resource allocations on a state level. Other states, for example New Hampshire, have demonstrated success in changing local and state policies and service networks to more effectively address the needs of elder abuse victims through the formation of statewide coalitions (Bergeron, 1989). Should a national coalition emerge, established local and state coalitions will have already developed the necessary structure and linkages to participate.

PROFESSIONAL TRAINING AND EDUCATION

The *New York Times* April 2 editorial issued a challenge to the social work profession to develop the interest and the expertise in working with elder abuse victims and their families. This is especially salient in view of recent research findings that unimpaired elders caring for impaired adult children are vulnerable to abuse. The mental health services provided by social workers can assist abusers who are impaired as well as elderly victims. It is also significant that in the Boston elder abuse study, findings showed that spouses predominated among abusers (Pillemer & Finkelhor, 1988). This is in line with the findings of a recent study by the New York City Department for the Aging of its elder abuse case load that 26% of the abusers were also elderly (Berman, 1990).

Schools of social work that emphasize gerontology services are in a position to take the lead in developing specialized curricula on elder abuse and interventions appropriate to this problem. This can enable social work schools to play a significant role in educating professional workers to take the lead in addressing the tragic and complex phenomenon of elder abuse. The case examples presented at the beginning of the chapter can be used to demonstrate how social workers' expertise, developed out of professional training, applies to elder abuse case intervention:

- The severely retarded son being cared for by his older parents was placed in a facility through the intervention of the parents' social worker, who was knowledgeable about the administrative structure of the state agency for the retarded. She contacted an administrator who understood the problem of elder abuse and had the authority to order the son placed out of his sequence on the waiting list in order to ensure the safety of his parents.
- Adult Protective Services (APS) was alerted in the case of

the elderly widow with the live-in housekeeper. An APS social worker arranged for an examination by a psychiatrist, who found the widow to be sufficiently judgment-impaired to warrant a court petition for a guardian. The APS social worker arranged for the removal of the housekeeper and, once the guardian was appointed by the court, worked with the guardian to develop a plan of care.

• In the case of the woman brought to the emergency room by her husband who said he accidently injured her, both husband and wife were hospitalized for treatment, then discharged to their home. As part of the discharge plan, the hospital social worker arranged for Medicaid benefits and home care, which enabled the couple to remain in the community. The hospital social worker also made a referral to a community-based social service agency, which assigned the couple to a social worker. She arranged for back rent and utilities to be paid, then identified supported housing for the couple, and made a referral to an agency providing day treatment and respite services to Alzheimer's patients and their families.

• The 85-year-old man whose son and his girlfriend had moved in with him accepted services from a social worker in his community who was trained in counseling elder abuse victims. However, while he acknowledged that he was being victimized by his son, he resisted holding his son responsible for his actions. The social worker, who understood the difficulties an elderly parent has in acknowledging abuse by an adult child, continued to work with him toward this goal. She also worked with the son to identify services for him through the Veteran's Hospital, knowing the father would be more amenable to accepting continued services if he knew efforts were being made to assist his son.

CONCLUSION

Rosalie Wolf notes in her 1988 article "Elder Abuse: Ten Years Later" that the efforts in the decade since Steinmetz first testified on elder abuse before the House Committee on Domestic Violence have seen a number of achievements.

Much more is known about the nature of familial relationships in later life, the risk factors that can precipitate violent or exploitative behavior against older family members, and the kind of interventions that have proven to be effective.

There has also been a coming together of many different kinds of professionals and others from all the various sectors—law enforcement, health care, mental health and, of course, the social work profession—who may come into contact with elder abuse victims to discuss how best to coordinate service efforts. Wolf concludes that with a continued commitment from the private and public sectors, the 1990s can bring greater progress in understanding and preventing elder abuse (Wolf, 1988).

Few professionals working with abuse victims would disagree with this assessment. Although a significant amount of research, training, and service development has taken place already, much is left to do. Unlike the decade of the 1980s, there is an agenda for the present decade, particularly for the social work profession. The challenge is to ensure that it is realized.

Abelman, I. (1992). *Report on incidence of adult abuse on the protective services for adults caseload in New York State.* Unpublished Report: New York State Department of Social Services.

American Association of Retired Persons. (1987). *Domestic maltreatment of the elderly: Towards prevention.* Criminal Justice Services Program Department (Pamphlet).

Anderson, J., & Theiss, J. (1989). Making policy research count: Elder abuse as a legislative issue. In R. Filinson & S. Ingman (Eds.), *Elder abuse: Practice and policy* (pp. 229–241). New York: Human Services Press.

Anetzberger, G. (1987). *The etiology of elder abuse by adult offspring.* Springfield, IL: Thomas.

Bergeron, L. (1989). Elder abuse and prevention: A holistic approach. In R. Filinson & S. Ingman (Eds.), *Elder abuse: Practice and policy* (pp. 218–228). New York: Human Services Press.

Berman, J. (1990). *Elder abuse: A profile of victims served by the New*

York City Department for the Aging. New York: Department for the Aging.

Breckman, R., & Adelman, R. (1988). *Strategies for helping victims of elder mistreatment.* Newbury Park, CA: Sage Press.

Brown, A. (1989). A survey on elder abuse among one Native American tribe. *Journal of Elder Abuse and Neglect, 1*(2), 17–37.

Burr, J. J. (1982). *Protective services for adults* (DHHS Publication No. [OHDS] 82–20505). Washington, DC: U.S. Department of Health and Human Services.

Butler, R. (1975). *Why survive? Being old in America.* New York: Harper & Row.

Callahan, J. (1988). Elder abuse: Some questions for policymakers. *The Gerontologist, 28*(4), 453–458.

Cantor, M. (1986). Strain among caregivers: A study of experience in the United States. In L. E. Troll (Ed.), *Family issues in current gerontology* (pp. 246–263). New York: Springer.

Cantor, M. (1991). Family and community: Changing roles in an aging society. *The Gerontologist, 31*(3), 337–346.

Crystal, S. (1987). Elder abuse: The latest crisis. *Public Interest, 88*(Summer), 56–66.

Faulkner, L. (1982). Mandating the reporting of suspected cases of elder abuse: An inappropriate, ineffective and ageist response to the abuse of older adults. *Family Law Quarterly, 16*(1), 69–91.

Filinson, R. (1989). Introduction. In R. Filinson & S. Ingman (Eds.), *Elder abuse: Practice and policy* (pp. 17–33). New York: Human Services Press.

Finkelhor, D., and Pillemer, K. (1988). Elder abuse: Its relationship to other forms of violence. In G. Hotaling, D, Finkelhor, J. Kirkpatrick, & M. Straus (Eds.), *Family abuse and its consequences: New directions in research* (pp. 244–254). Newbury Park, CA: Sage.

Fulmer, T., & O'Malley, T. (1987). *Inadequate care of the elderly: A health care perspective on abuse and neglect.* New York: Springer.

Griffin, L. W., & Williams, O. J. (1992). Abuse among African–American elderly. *Journal of Family Violence, 7*(1), 19–35.

Help for the Terrified Elderly. (1991, April 2) *New York Times,* editorial.

Hickey, T., and Douglass, R. (1981). Neglect and abuse of elder family members: Professionals' perspectives and case experiences. *The Gerontologist, 21*(2), 171–176.

Hudson, M. (1986). Elder mistreatment: Current research. In K. Pillemer & R. Wolf (Eds.), *Elder abuse: Conflict in the family* (pp. 125–166). Dover, MA: Auburn House.

Johnson, T. (1986). Critical issues in the definition of elder mis-treatment. In K. Pillemer & R. Wolf (Eds.), *Elder abuse: Conflict in the family*. Dover, MA: Auburn House.

Kinderknecht, C. (1986). In-home social work with abused or neglected elderly: An experiential guide to assessment and treatment. *Journal of Gerontological Social Work, 9*(3), 29–42.

King, N. (1984). Exploitation and abuse of older family members: An overview of the problem. In J. Costa (Ed.), *Abuse of the elderly: A guide to resources and services* (pp. 3–12). Lexington, MA: Lexington Books.

Missouri Department of Social Services, Division of Aging (1981). Handout.

Pillemer, K. and Finkelhor, D. (1988). The prevalence of elder abuse: A random sample survey. *The Gerontologist, 28*(1), 51–57.

Pillemer, K. & Finkelhor, D. (1989). Causes of elder abuse: Care-giver versus problem relatives. *American Orthopsychiatric Association, 59*(2), 179–187.

Quinn, M., & Tomita, S. (1986). *Elder abuse and neglect*. New York: Springer.

Reinharz, S. (1986). Loving and hating one's elders: Twin themes in legend and literature. In K. Pillemer & R. Wolf (Eds.), *Elder abuse: Conflict in the family* (pp. 25–47). Dover, MA: Auburn House.

Rinkle, V. (1989). Federal initiatives. In R. Filinson & S. Ingram (Eds.), *Elder abuse: Practice and policy issues* (pp. 129–137). New York: Human Services Press.

Steinmetz, S., Straus, M., & Gelles, R. (1980). *Behind closed doors*. Garden City, NY: Doubleday Anchor.

U.S. House of Representatives, Select Committee on Aging (1989). *Elder abuse: An assessment of the Federal response*. Washington, DC: U.S. Government Printing Office.

U.S. House of Representatives, Select Committee on Aging (1990). *Elder abuse: A decade of shame*. Washington, DC: U.S. Government Printing Office.

Vinton, L. (1992). Battered women's shelters and older women: The Florida experience. *Journal of Family Violence, 7*(1), 63–72.

Wolf, R. (1988). Elder abuse: Ten years later. *Journal of the American Geriatric Society, 10*(8), 758–762.

Wolf, R., & Pillemer, K. (1984). *Working with abused elderly: Assessment, advocacy and intervention*. Wooster, MA: University of Massachusetts Medical Center, University Center on Aging.

6

Social Work and Bioethics: Ethical Issues in Long–Term-Care Practice

Bart Collopy and Martha C. Bial

EARLY SOCIAL WORK GERONTOLOGISTS were keenly aware of the ethical dilemmas inherent in providing care to dependent adults in nursing homes and community-based programs (Blenkner, 1965; Wasser, 1966), but discussion of these dilemmas remained largely internal to the field of social work and sparked little exchange with the other professions serving long-term care. This lack of dialogue could be traced in part to the insulating effect of professional languages and methodologies; in part, to a practice-based stratification that made medical and non-medical professionals wary of each other.

In the late 1960s, bioethics began to foster an interdisciplinary approach to health care ethics, but the emerging dialogue rarely included the perspective of social work. Bioethics was overwhelmingly concerned with the problems of acute care medicine and biomedical research (e.g., life-sustaining treatment, the care of impaired newborns, organ transplants, genetic experimentation, reproductive technology). As a result, the emerging bioethics discussion paid scant attention to long-term care and was all but silent about the ethical dilemmas that social workers faced in nursing homes and community-based services to the elderly. To the extent that there was discussion of long–term-care ethics, it continued to take place within the separate professions serving long-term care.

Fortunately for both bioethics and social work, the ethical isolation of long-term care shows clear signs of change. Bioethics has begun to look at long-term care and its distinctive issues. At the same time, there has been a surge of recent interest in bioethical issues from within *and across* the various professions serving the elderly (*The Gerontologist*, 1988; *Generations*, 1990).

The following discussion is an attempt to contribute to the emerging dialogue, particularly between ethicists, social workers, physicians, and nurses. Our discussion begins with an overview of bioethical issues that social workers confront in long–term-care settings. To bring these issues into the world of practice, we present next a number of brief case studies. In the commentary that follows these cases, we have avoided separate "ethicist" and "social worker" perspectives and have tried to develop a common response, to show at least one social worker and one ethicist "doing ethics" across their disciplines. Throughout the discussion, our intent is not to provide answers to the dilemmas of long–term-care ethics, but to explore these dilemmas, to suggest common terminology, concepts, and modes of analysis, to offer strategies that might be useful on the way to answers.

AN OVERVIEW OF THE ISSUES

Life-Sustaining Treatment

In terms of moral drama, the most riveting issues in long-term care are those that involve life-sustaining medical treatment. As an unabating stream of court cases indicates, decisions to forgo or discontinue medical treatment at the edges of life continue to be perplexing and conflictual (Colby et al., 1990; Cranford, Rie, Ackerman, & Callahan, 1991). What is the proper response when an elderly person (or that person's surrogate) refuses a respirator, or dialysis, or antibiotics? How should "Do Not Resuscitate" orders be formulated, or "Do Not Hospitalize" orders? And what should guide decision making about the most contentious issue in end-of-life medicine: the use of feeding tubes (Lynn, 1986; Kayser-Jones, 1990; Scofield, 1991)?

These questions about forms of treatment lead inevitably

to questions about decision-makers and decision-making processes. *Who* should participate in these decisions, for example? What process ensures the best kind of participation? In cases of conflict, who should be the *primary* decision-maker? Who should have the last word? And how should advance directives ensure this last word for those who are mentally incapacitated? Finally, of course, the elemental question: What is the *right* decision in any one particular case? What moral calculus should balance benefits and burdens, sanctity of life and quality of life, ordinary and extraordinary levels of care (President's Commission, 1983; Hastings Center, 1989; Cohen, 1988).

At first glance, these questions might seem to define specifically *medical* terrain. But even though medical expertise and advice are essential to the decision-making process, decisions to accept or refuse treatment are primarily moral, value-based decisions, not medical ones. And in the decision-making process, non-medical staff members can be crucial to patients and their families.

This is especially true in long-term care. Social workers, for example, often have long-standing contact with elderly residents and clients. Sometimes their involvement in a particular case dates back to an elderly person's placement in a nursing home or home-care program. As a result, they may know the individual's values and preferences and may be able to mediate with family members far better than physicians whose contact with a patient may be very recent and limited to medical matters.

Ideally, questions about life-sustaining treatment should be raised well in advance of emergency situations. And here social workers can play a crucial role, informing the elderly of their rights and options, eliciting their wishes, protecting their interests, counseling and educating family members, serving as intermediaries with physicians (who may be reluctant to raise terminal-care issues).

Other Treatment Issues

The complex issues and conflicts that can develop around life-sustaining treatment are generally recognized. In fact, they may seem, at times, to constitute the major concern of bioethics. As a result, even providers of long-term care may be inclined to overlook the ethical tangles within more ordinary forms of care. Yet these ordinary arenas of care, even though they may summon up less moral drama, are the basic stuff of long-term care, defining its day-to-day environment and producing their own variety of moral dilemmas.

Non-compliance with care is the clearest and most difficult of these day-to-day dilemmas. An elderly woman in home care might take her blood pressure medication irregularly, or might refuse hospitalization for a serious foot infection related to a diabetic condition. An elderly man in a nursing home might balk at physical therapy after a hip fracture or refuse to follow a special diet. The harm resulting from such refusals can range from minimal to serious. But whatever the harm, non-compliance raises questions not only about the rights of individuals to refuse care, but also about the obligations of care providers to respect a client's autonomous "no."

Behavioral Problems

Beyond refusals of medical care, there exists another range of "non-compliance" rarely found in acute care but quite common in nursing homes and community settings: harmful, disruptive, or socially aberrant behavior. Frail elderly may fall frequently; they may wander into stairwells or out into busy street traffic. They may turn physically threatening, verbally abusive, noisy, intrusive on others. They may fail to eat properly. Their physical care of themselves may deteriorate. In countless ways, they may become socially "unseemly," less and less able to manage basic daily activities, to sustain the order and dignity of their past lives.

Confronted with these risks and diminishments, social workers face decisions about protecting, constraining, or otherwise managing the life and choices of their clients. Often the question that surfaces is one of transferring clients to different or more intensive care-settings. Such transfers generally increase the authority of caregivers and constrain the elderly person's autonomy and independence.

In extreme cases, there may be pressures to seek involuntary institutionalization of the elderly person or a court-ordered guardianship (Iris, 1988, 1990; Coleman and Dooley, 1990). Within institutional settings, there may be pressures to use physical or pharmacological restraints to "manage" dangerous or disruptive behavior (Collopy, 1992).

In all these instances, the autonomy, dignity, and privacy of the individual stand poised against the "values of intervention": safety, the obligation to pursue the client's best interests, and the common good. Here social workers routinely face dilemmas and difficult choices—choices made no easier by the social mores and professional biases that run inescapably beneath any discussion of *behavioral* problems.

Unsafe Settings and Care Plans

In community settings social workers can find clients living under conditions that are unclean, unsafe, or simply inadequate to meet the needs of frailty and decent caregiving. But elderly individuals often resist attempts to change these conditions, viewing suggested "improvements" as invasions of their privacy or lifestyle. Even when they receive inadequate care or suffer outright neglect and abuse, some elderly will reject interventions that are meant to protect them. Such situations can be further complicated by value dissonance, by the hard fact that elderly clients and social workers do not always share companionable value systems. What seems risky to a care provider can seem routine to a client. If there is wide discrepancy of this sort, a case can simply curdle with dilemmas about client freedom, professional responsibility, the rights and obligations of the caring agency, the role of protective services, regulators, and even the courts.

Of course, not all problems with care plans and care settings result from incongruence between the values of clients and care providers. Many of the problems are systemic in source, presenting situations in which clients and caregivers together face the stringencies of the health care system—limits on the length and nature of covered services, the high costs of private home care, and the difficulties of access to and coordination among multiple service providers, between formal and informal caregivers. Minimal training, high turnover, and instances of unreliability among home-care aides create additional systemic problems.

In fact, while a resistant *client* can raise problems, social workers may feel that the resistant health care *system* is a far greater and more powerful source of ethical dilemmas. Medicare's prospective payment system, for example, presses for quick hospital discharge of elderly patients, even though nursing home beds are scarce and coverage for home-care services is tightly limited. These systemic conditions lead to forced choices, produce care plans lean in services, and leave care providers with the discomforting justification that "some care is better than none." Thus, the barest cupboard of home-care services may seem better than institutionalization. Or, conversely and no less questionably, institutionalization may seem necessary because available services in the community are inadequate and the nursing home, despite the client's objections, is at least a safe place.

Institutional Settings

Nursing home placement brings, of course, its own distinctive set of ethical problems. Every nursing home is, at least potentially, a "total institution," to use Goffman's (1961) term for environments that exercise powerful control and containment over their residents or inmates. As total institutions, nursing homes are places where the elderly lose significant control over many areas of self-determined living: daily schedule, choice of food, choice of roommates and tablemates, of entertainment and leisure, of personalized surroundings and of room arrangements, and even of one's own chair (Kane & Caplan, 1990; Lidz & Arnold, 1990; Johnson & Grant, 1985). On the other hand, managed living is to some extent inescapable when many frail individuals live in common, and choices are bound to be circumscribed when the resources of a nursing home are necessarily limited. In short, the freedoms of adult life in a private dwelling cannot be fully replicated in a nursing home.

But the inescapable limits of institutional life ought to be distinguished from those that are imposed for the sake of institutional efficiency, "paper compliance" with regulations, or profit-margin motives. A commitment to counter the depersonalizing and dependency-nurturing aspects of institutional care would call, then, for "deinstitutionalizing" the nursing home, creating opportunities for residents to exercise personal choice and to escape "batch handling" as much as possible. But this approach to care can rattle the routines of institutional life, and social workers trying to make an institution less "total" may find themselves in crossfire between the residents and the institution, even between residents themselves when their freer choices and lifestyles collide.

Burdens on Informal Caregivers

For many of the frail elderly who live at home, family members and other informal caregivers supply large amounts of direct care and care management. Despite the designation of this care as "informal," it often takes a heavy toll on caregivers. Moreover, under the pressure of a hospital discharge or a desire to avoid institutionalizing a family member, informal caregivers can overestimate their own resources *and* underestimate the burdens they are assuming. The consequent strains on informal caregivers inevitably touch professionals, especially case managers, who must work with family members and others to ensure ongoing quality care for clients.

In such situations, social workers must often take on complex interventions, mediating conflicts between the elderly and their family caregivers, helping families to admit that they have reached end points, that they have to seek more assistance or even consider institutional placement of their elderly relative. To the extent that families carry the burdens of home care, they deserve some voice in decisions affecting that care. But there is no set formula for gauging the extent of this voice. While recognizing the "extended cliency" of the family, social workers still face obligations to the elderly person as primary client.

This complex balancing of rights and interests is made more difficult by a reimbursement system that does not cover service, counseling, and education given to family members—even though this kind of contact with family members can have immense payoffs in terms of quality of care. Again, the ironies of the health care system are painfully heavy-handed. The reimbursement system follows an abstracted, "isolated client" view of care while those on the front line struggle to help elderly individuals who are often deeply enmeshed in familial relationships.

Politics and Practicalities

In the often gritty reality of social work, all the above problems involve politics and practicalities as well as ethical principles. The "politics" of providing services to the elderly means meshing effectively with supervisors and coworkers, with outside agencies, with families and other advocates of elderly clients. In fact, this meshing or "getting along" within an organization is itself an ethical imperative. The NASW Code of Ethics says that the "social worker should cooperate with colleagues to promote professional interests and concerns, . . . should work to improve the employing agency's policies and procedures, and the efficiency and effectiveness of its services" (Loewenberg & Dolgoff, 1988, pp. 147, 149).

The art of politics calls for pursuing ethical principles and policies with a clear eye on the power structures that shape any given situation or decision. There are certainly occasions when an unyielding stand on principle is the only validly ethical response, but in the day-to-day business of serving clients, ethical problems call for responses that are workable as well as principled. Thus, social workers may not always choose to challenge the structures of power immediately, directly, or single-handedly on behalf of a client or an ethical principle. The political reality of a given situation may call for negotiation and alliance-building. Incremental advocacy may prove more effective than "all-or-nothing" confrontation; a moral stand that is contagious rather than isolated is liable to have the deepest impact on institutional and agency policy.

SOME ILLUSTRATIVE CASES

To illustrate the way ethical issues present a mix of principles, politics, and practicalities, we present below a number of cases that display the range of ethical questions that can arise in social work practice in long-term care, questions about autonomy, the limits of confidentiality, the definition of *primary client*, the rights of families as secondary clients, the tension between client rights and staff rights, between client wishes and agency resources.[1]

Case I

Mary and William Adler are private paying residents of the Spring Gardens Nursing Home. They are housed on separate floors because Mr. Adler suffers from multi-infarct dementia and is physically very frail. His wife has a chronic heart condition, but is quite alert and independent-minded, and could have continued living in the community had she not chosen to enter the home to be with her husband.

The social worker believes that Mrs. Adler's desire not to be separated from her husband contains a strong element of control. In fact, the couple's psychosocial history indicates that she has always been the decision-maker in the family, with Mr. Adler deferring to her wishes.

At Spring Gardens, Mr. Adler has a roommate who is confused, incontinent, and disruptive. Mr. Adler has never complained about this, but his wife has requested a room change for her husband, claiming that his present roommate is "absolutely unbearable."

In due course another bed becomes available, and Mrs. Adler presses for an immediate change of room for her husband. When the social worker visits him to discuss this, Mr. Adler's conversation is rambling and occasionally disoriented, but the social worker feels that he understands exactly what is at stake and that he is not at all inclined to move.

When the social worker reports this conversation to Mrs. Adler, she vehemently tells him that her husband is far too confused to make a decision of this sort. "I don't want to discuss this any further," she finally says. "I simply want his room changed."

Immediately after this conversation, the nursing home administrator meets the social worker and presses him to resolve the question of reassigning Mr. Adler as soon as possible so that the empty bed can be filled.

The social worker decides to bring Mr. Adler to visit his potential roommate. After the visit, Mr. Adler tells the social worker that he has seen this man urinate in the corner of the television room and, on another occasion, throw his cane at another resident. He also has a sharp memory of the man being "nasty" to him in the dining room. Again, getting this response from Mr. Adler is difficult and time consuming, but the social worker is convinced that he prefers his present roommate.

The social worker relays the whole incident to Mrs. Adler and tells her that he has decided not to transfer her husband. He feels that Mr. Adler clearly does not want the change. Mrs. Adler is appalled. "I can't believe you're letting my husband make such a decision," she says. "He is in no condition to know what he wants or doesn't want."

This case raises a number of issues that loom large and vexing in long–term-care ethics: decisional capacity, surrogate decision making, and the definition of primary client. The presence of dementia and other forms of cognitive deficit among elderly clients raises obvious questions about their capacity to gauge risks and make informed choices. In short, diminished capacity can mean diminished autonomy and a consequent dependency on others to act as their surrogates or proxies. The most obvious candidates for the surrogates are, of course, family members, but determining when exactly surrogates should step in can be a difficult task—and one that holds high risks for the autonomy of the elderly.

Inadequate assessments of competency often result from failure to recognize that decisional capacity can be intermittent and fluctuating and that it should always be evaluated in terms of *specific* abilities or areas of judgment. The specificity of decisional capacity is particularly crucial because it warns against blanket or global assessments of incapacity, except in the extreme stages of dementia.

As the above case suggests, an elderly individual may be incapacitated in some areas of decision making but sufficiently capable in others. Drawing these boundaries can be a difficult task, however. Communication problems can add to the difficulty and even mistakenly suggest mental incapacity. Assessments can be further harried by discharge and transfer pressures as well as by interventions from family members. For this reason, it is crucial for long–term-care institutions and agencies to set consistent standards for assessing capacity. This requires formal policies (and staff education) that would work against stereotypic and impressionistic judgments of mental ability; "tests" of mental status that are at best initial screenings and not in-depth diagnosis; and reliance on medical status (e.g., "multi-infarct dementia") as categorical proof of incapacity (President's Commission, 1982; Tancredi, 1987).

At the very least, such policies can inject caution and care into assessments of incapacity. More positively, they can encourage efforts to develop profiles of the wishes and preferences of the elderly. In this regard, a particularly useful approach is the use of a "values history" which asks not only about preferences for end-of-life treatment, but also about the underlying life values and personal perspectives that might inform the whole range of medical and psychosocial care (McCullough, 1984; Gibson, 1990).

A values history can often be helpful in assessing decisional capacity, because it provides a norm for assessing the deeper characterological coherence of choices, particularly idiosyncratic choices. Moreover, when clients are severely incapacitated, these histories provide powerful guidance for surrogate decision making, enabling proxies to speak as much as possible in the voice of the elderly individual rather than in their own voice or in the abstractions of a general "best interest" standard.

A crucial political issue underlies this whole discussion: the need for policies that *institutionalize* ethics while preserving the moral agency of individual clients and professionals. Good institutional policy should accomplish this by shaping a corporate milieu in which the individual professional exercises moral discretion yet does not have to chart a lonely and isolated course in dealing with ethical dilemmas.

In the above case, for example, a policy on the "ethics of capacity and consent" would support the social worker's struggle to determine the real reach of Mr. Adler's autonomy, especially in the face of his wife's pressure and Mr. Adler's communication problems. While family members generally make the most effective surrogates, immediate deference to them as surrogates can be ethically naïve. Families are not always dependable barometers of an elderly person's capacities or preferences. They may react paternalistically or become so distressed by an elderly relative's disabilities that they fail to recognize decisional capacities and autonomous preferences that continue in the midst of these disabilities. Long-standing personal conflicts, patterns of control, sudden reversals in authority and dependency, can all further distort a family's ability to speak in the voice of an elderly relative.

In the context of family surrogacy, then, the issue of decisional capacity often raises the question "Who is the client?" If the social worker sees *both* Mr. and Mrs. Adler as his clients, then his focus, indeed his ethical obligation, would be to sustain the autonomy of both parties and try to help them resolve their differences. Since Mrs. Adler is convinced that her husband is decisionally incapacitated, mediating a common understanding between them could be a long and arduous task. And fiscal pressures to fill the empty bed will certainly work against long-term mediation.

Pressed to act expeditiously, the social worker might be tempted to adopt a family systems solution that accepts Mrs. Adler's long-time role as decision-maker for the couple. Her dominance could be further ratified by her status as the manager of the couple's finances, the "payer" who negotiates such things as room assignments.

It could be argued that this "solution" thoroughly bypasses Mr. Adler's autonomy, that it reduces a moral judgment ("Who is the client?") to an economic one ("Who is the payer?"). In any case, the social worker rejects this approach. He clearly sees Mr. Adler as the primary client—and one who is competent to make this particular decision. Even if Mr. Adler generally does go along with his wife's decisions, he might not *always* do so, and he should therefore be consulted about a decision that holds potentially high stakes for him.

Of course, the problem is not resolved by determining that Mr. Adler is sufficiently autonomous to refuse a change of room. Even if Mrs. Adler is not the primary client, she is his surrogate in areas where he is not autonomous. More simply and practically, she is his wife, and the decision of the social worker to support Mr. Adler against her wishes could stir trouble in the couple's relationship, in her role as surrogate in other matters, and in her wider relationship to the institution and its staff.

Thus, as often happens in the family unit, a resolution at one point stirs a problem elsewhere. In deciding to support Mr. Adler's autonomy, the social worker now has the task of easing possible strains in the relationship between Mr. and Mrs. Adler, of not leaving Mrs. Adler with the feeling that she has been displaced as surrogate for her husband.

In this case, the social worker can appeal to Mrs. Adler's concern for her husband's welfare. He can recount the visit, point out that the new roommate is liable to bring new problems for her husband—and quite possibly a request for still another room change. In other words he can validate Mrs. Adler's concerns and at the same time press her to reconsider her demand. In the end, the ethical make-up of the case calls for more than giving primacy to Mr. Adler's autonomy. The best resolution would resist Mrs. Adler's control but, at the same time, respect her basic concern for her husband and sustain her role as surrogate in other areas.

Case II

Mrs. Brooks, an elderly widow who lives alone in her own apartment, receives twenty hours a week of home-care assistance and additional care from various family members living nearby. She is a patient in a geriatric medical group, and at a routine visit she confides to the social worker that her home health aide has hit her. She shows the social worker a noticeable bruise on her upper arm, but when asked if she has reported the incident she says she does not want to get involved in "anything like that." The social worker presses the issue, and Mrs. Brooks, afraid that the social worker might unilaterally file a complaint, pleads with her to keep silence. Despite this recent incident, she has had less trouble with this aide than with any other sent to her from the agency. "I don't know who they'll send me if I complain. At least this aide shows up on time and doesn't smoke and blast the radio like the last one. And she doesn't steal. I'm better off with her."

Uneasy with this case, the social worker talks with Mrs. Brooks's physician who describes his patient as a demanding woman who might have provoked the aide. After a lengthy discussion, the social worker and the physician decide that Mrs. Brooks is competent to make this decision, that the injury she sustained is limited, and that they should respect her wish not to pursue the incident with her family or the home-care agency.

This case counterposes two sets of values: client autonomy and confidentiality, on one side, beneficent care and professional responsibility to protect a vulnerable elderly person, on the other (Reamer, 1982). One's immediate, intuitive ranking of these values may be colored by professional setting. Presented with this case, social workers from Adult Protective Services saw it as instance of abuse—which the social worker had a clear duty to report. In their eyes, Mrs. Brooks's reference to the incident was a cry for help, an indirect attempt to "report" what had happened. Social workers from other practice settings were more inclined to respect Mrs. Brooks's request not to report the incident. They saw her conversation with the social worker as a sign of a positive relationship which allowed her to tell her story, receive sympathy and support, and trust that her account would go no further.

The response of the Protective Services' staff clearly affirms beneficence, the principle that obligates care providers to protect clients from harm. This obligation is especially sharp when clients are frail and defenseless, when their vulnerability is heightened by the "closeted" setting of home care, and when the abuse comes from someone who works under the auspices and direct control of the home-care agency. Moreover, the definition of "client" extends here beyond Mrs. Brooks to other elderly who might be subject to abuse from this aide.

The strong presumption for protective action becomes problematic, however, when the client requests (*pleads*, actually) that the mistreatment not be reported. Should confidentiality override beneficence in this case? Does the request for confidentiality outweigh the risk Mrs. Brooks will continue to face from the aide? Is there anything in the nature of her request which would qualify or diminish its binding quality?

Impairment of mental capacity would of course undercut such a request. But Mrs. Brooks appears to be fully competent, and so considerations of mental capacity do not ease this particular dilemma. (It is worth noting how morally "relieving" an assessment of incapacity can be in a case of this sort. To the extent that Mrs. Brooks is judgmentally impaired, the force of her request for confidentiality lessens. Precisely because a diagnosis of mental impairment can so easily solve some moral dilemmas, there may be an underlying bias toward such assessments.)

Because Mrs. Brooks is competent, her moral account of the case, her weighing of benefits and burdens, must be taken seriously. As she sees it, the risk of additional physical abuse is outweighed by the positive qualities in this aide and the negative experience she has had (and anticipates) with other aides.

In support of Mrs. Brooks's view, it does seem that this is an isolated incident and one that did not result in serious injury. Moreover, Mrs. Brooks's request for confidentiality is a request that her autonomy be respected, that she be allowed to take a risk she finds preferable to supposedly "safer," but otherwise unsatisfactory, care from other aides. In this analysis, it would be hard to find the "compelling professional reasons" which the NASW Code of Ethics requires as a justification to breach client confidentiality (Loewenberg & Dolgoff, 1988).

On the other hand, while a case can be made for honoring Mrs. Brooks's confidentiality, the obligation to protect a client from physical mistreatment is a strong one and should not easily cede to generalities assuring us that "even good aides occasionally lose their patience." On balance, the decision to respect Mrs. Brooks's autonomy might be defensible, but the obligation to protect her should not be quickly set aside. Professional beneficence—the social worker's concern for the best interests of this client—would call for close attention to the progress of the case. At the very least, the social worker ought to explore Mrs. Brooks's understanding of the risks she is facing. It would also be crucial to negotiate an understanding that the social worker will keep in touch with her about her ongoing relationship with this aide. In short, *guarded* acquiescence to Mrs. Brooks's request may be the course of action that most fully respects her autonomy, honors her request for confidence, and admits a continuing professional obligation to protect her.

The physician's comment that Mrs. Brooks "may have provoked the aide" is somewhat speculative and, in any case, does not excuse the mistreatment. On the other hand, the physician does raise the possibility that the incident was impulsive, not a deliberate act by a characterologically hostile aide. Discreet inquiries in the agency about the aide's relationship with other clients, and about Mrs Brooks's dealings with other aides, might also be pursued. Here, the practical strategies for getting an accurate reading of the case will vary, depending on the agency and the social worker's collegial network.

A tough realism about this case might also suggest that Mrs. Brooks was struck by someone else, perhaps a family member whom she is protecting. While the case presents no facts to substantiate this possibility, we do know that in elder abuse, as in other forms of domestic violence, victims often do not complain because they are too ashamed, too fearful of retaliation, or too dependent on the relationship with the abuser.

It might be appropriate, then, for the social worker to probe the nature of the family situation. Breckman and Adelman (1988) have developed helpful guidelines for detecting the presence of elder abuse and determining the appropriate intervention. If there is reason to suspect abuse, then those states with mandated reporting laws would require a formal complaint from the social worker. However, unless harm or threat to life seems imminent, the social worker should first attempt to gain the client's permission for disclosure. This would be in line with Loewenberg and Dolgoff's (1988) ranking of ethical principles. A client's right to confidentiality would rank above the social worker's obligation to disclose, but below the client's right to survival.

Assuming that Mrs. Brooks's account is not shielding a more serious problem, the social worker's response is ethically justifiable. In terms of the dynamics of this case, it is worth noting that the social worker is more ready to trust Mrs. Brooks's judgment after her discussion with the physician. The case thus indicates how much institutions and agencies need collegial strategies, even formal processes (ethics committees, specific policies, for example), for the resolution of ethical problems (Conrad, 1989). In the absence of such collective response, an agency simply leaves its staff members to navigate difficult moral straits on their own, with possible damage to moral consistency within the agency's practice.

Collegial response raises, of course, its own complexities.

In this case, for example, it might be argued that the social worker in sharing Mrs. Brooks's story with her physician has already violated confidentiality. Although there is some merit to this argument, the social worker *does* honor Mrs. Brooks's explicit request not to report the incident. Moreover, as an agency employee, she has a duty to share critical information with colleagues who may also be held accountable for Mrs. Brooks's safety. The most balanced response here might be for the social worker to ask Mrs. Brooks if she can discuss the matter, confidentially, with the treating physician.

Consultation with colleagues may in fact provide greater support to a social worker who wants to respect a client's dilemma-laden request. A professional worried about personal or agency liability might be fearful of proceeding entirely on her own in a case of this sort. The result may be a premature decision to protect a client rather then respect her autonomy.

Case III

Mrs. Crimmins, an alert, fully competent, but extremely disabled amputee, lives with her only companion, a large unruly dog, in an apartment that the worker from Adult Protective Services describes as "incredibly cluttered and dirty." Mrs. Crimmins is unable to do much cooking or take care of her apartment. (A neighbor walks the dog, occasionally.) But despite her limitations, she refuses to discuss a nursing home placement. Reluctant to force this issue, Adult Protective Services requests home attendant service from Elderhelp, a local home-care agency. The social worker who visits from Elderhelp realizes that this will be a difficult case, but the agency develops a care plan for four hours per day of home-care service. The first attendant who visits the apartment is appalled by its condition and fearful of the dog who is constantly menacing. When Mrs. Crimmins tells her she must take the dog for a walk, the attendant refuses. An argument ensues, the attendant leaves, and immediately informs her supervisor that she simply cannot work on this case.

A social worker from the agency visits and tries to find some compromise, suggesting that Mrs. Crimmins have her apartment cleaned and that she restrain her dog during the home attendant's presence. Mrs. Crimmins is uncooperative, insisting that she is satisfied with the apartment as it is and that she won't be forced to spend money on a cleaning service "to satisfy your workers." "I need help, and you shouldn't refuse it because you don't like my apartment or my dog," she tells the social worker.

Soon after, the case reaches an impasse. Additional visits to Mrs. Crimmins produce no compromise and Elderhelp is unable to find an attendant willing to work under the existing conditions. The agency informs Protective Services that it cannot provide services. The social worker who has handled the case so far speculates that Protective Services will contact other home-care agencies and that Mrs. Crimmins will become a "problem client," shuttled from agency to agency. "Protective Services is liable to come back, soon enough, and ask us to try again."

Community-based care of the elderly has many attractions over institutional care, especially in its ability to sustain the independence, privacy, accustomed lifestyles, and social contexts of the elderly. But care in the community also has its distinctive problems (as the deinstitutionalization of mental health care has made dramatically clear). Not all elderly clients thrive at home. It may be impossible to provide the required level of care; their home settings may be unsafe; their lifestyles may effectively void the care they receive; their basic expectations about care may prove irreconcilable with the resources or professional standards of care providers. Since social workers play a strategic role in matching clients with services, they must often struggle with any "lack of fit" between the elderly and community-based care.

Client autonomy is often a central ethical issue in such cases. In principle, home care aims at providing services that support rather than erode the elderly individual's autonomy. Ideally, then, good care meshes the professional goals and standards of the home-care agency with the personal preferences and living arrangements of those it serves. This accommodation is one of the hallmarks of home care. As the case of Mrs. Crimmins suggests, it can sometimes be one of its horrors.

Placement of Mrs. Crimmins in a nursing home would clearly have to be an involuntary placement and an ethically dubious one at present, since she appears to be competent. Of course, no one has thus far suggested such a placement. On the other hand, the question of involuntary commitment looms at the edges of this case; it will become more central if effective home care cannot be established and if Mrs. Crimmins' physical or mental condition diminishes. One of the components of the case is, therefore, its ethically troubling drift—the possibility that Mrs. Crimmins will move through a series of failed home-care placements until involuntary institutionalization becomes legally and morally plausible. In the end, temporizing may produce a kind of "resolution by deterioration." The prospect of such a resolution raises critical questions about the *overall* responsibility for this case and about the need for concerted intervention. At the very least, efforts should be made to convince Mrs. Crimmins that she faces a real risk of institutionalization if a workable care plan cannot be developed.

The prospect of involuntary placement, which *none* of those involved wants, dramatizes the moral ambiguity that often accompanies protective service cases. Providing care to the frail elderly and at the same time respecting their autonomy, local habitations, lifestyles, families, neighbors, even pets, can be a dilemma-ridden undertaking. Care providers may feel that a case will become tractable only when it becomes more tragic, for example, when Mrs. Crimmins' health deteriorates to the point that she is decisionally or physically so incapacitated that she becomes a clear and grave danger to herself.

For the present, however, she is competent and autonomous. Since she is at home, on her own turf, her autonomy may even be "emboldened" (Collopy, Dubler, & Zuckerman, 1990). She wants to control the terms of care, set the rules for it, be free of any requirement to clean her house or curb her dog in exchange for assistance. She grants no validity to the agency's concerns about safe and sanitary working conditions. But the acceptance of home-care services implies some willingness to adjust to the health care providers and the routines of care. Although the autonomy of clients and the privacy of their homes is a primary value, it is not an absolute and unconditional value.

Moreover, workers' rights are real even if they are less extensive than the rights of domestic privacy. And this points to another major issue raised by this case. Home-care aides and attendants often bear the brunt of home care, providing basic services to clients who may be severely frail, mentally impaired, unable to communicate, openly hostile, or excessively demanding. While there are instances of negligent care and even abuse from home-care attendants, they are also victims of abuse and mistreatment from clients and their families. Given their working conditions—low pay, minimal benefits, meager advancement opportunities, assignments that keep changing and often require traveling to multiple clients—attendants and aides are a hard-pressed if not exploited workforce (Zuckerman, 1990). Social workers who act as intermediaries between these workers and home-care clients have a significant responsibility to ensure decent working conditions for them. Thus, the social worker's role as negotiator once again brings ethical tension, in this case a tension between obligations to a client and obligations to other employees of the home-care agency.

In her role as intermediary, the social worker in this case tries to work out a "negotiated consent" (Moody, 1988) in which Mrs. Crimmins would agree to have her house cleaned and her dog controlled. Although negotiation fails, it remains from both practical and ethical perspectives the most workable strategy in cases of this sort. Attempting to resolve the conflict by giving priority to *one* set of rights or obligations (client autonomy or agency/worker rights, for example) would oversimplify the conflict and most likely not provide a workable solution.

The principal question that might be pressed at this point

would be whether the search for accommodation has been exhausted. In her refusal to cooperate, does Mrs. Crimmins intend in effect to refuse care from the agency? Does she realize the full import of this refusal—that she may preserve her autonomy in the short term, only to lose it in the long term? Would continuing discussion bring about some workable compromises? Are there accommodations which the home-care agency might make in this case? Would some minimal changes in the setting provide an initially manageable, even if not fully desirable, arrangement for a home-care attendant?

Through sustained contact, the social worker may help Mrs. Crimmins make a more fully informed choice, help her see that some accommodation in her living situation would bring her the care that she wants. On the other hand, Mrs. Crimmins may be unwilling to bend. Her refusal *may* be the equivalent of someone's refusing a particular medical treatment. If so, the social worker can only "leave the door open," hoping that Mrs. Crimmins may return to negotiate with the agency if her attempts to get home help on her terms are not successful.

Case IV

Miss Green is a long-time resident of the Pine Wood Nursing Home. She is an inveterate smoker, but she is also blind, and the new Director of Nursing feels strongly that a blind smoker is a severe safety hazard. Consequently, she determines that Miss Green may smoke only when a staff member can be with her.

The social worker at Pine Wood is convinced that Miss Green only needs someone to light her cigarettes, that she is able to manage by herself, using the ashtray appropriately and safely. But for the time being at least, the monitored smoking requirement stands. The home is short-staffed and experiences a steady influx of patients requiring heavy physical care. The result is that Miss Green has fewer and fewer opportunities to smoke.

As a result, she becomes increasingly hostile, verbally

aggressive and abusive to staff. She tries to enlist other residents to help her smoke "secretly," and she demands constant meetings with the Director of Nursing who, she says, is denying her her basic rights. There is little headway in these face-to-face sessions. Miss Green argues that she is being denied freedom of choice allowed to sighted residents. The Director of Nursing defends her decision in the name of Miss Green's own safety and the safety of everyone else at the home. "Besides," she says, "smoking is absolutely no good for your health."

In terms of the principles at stake, this case pits individual rights against the common good. If the Director of Nursing is correct in her assessment of risk, the threat of harm to others counters Miss Green's freedom to smoke. There is a question of justice or equity which also runs through this case. With a shortage of nursing staff, it might be argued that an aide cannot be often assigned to provide a "luxury" service for one resident.

The crucial element in this case is, of course, the Nursing Director's appeal to safety, an appeal that is frequently used to constrain individual choice—and for that very reason an appeal that deserves close scrutiny. In long-term care, a good deal of the emphasis on safety can be traced to regulatory requirements, but such requirements can elevate safety over other values in rather doctrinaire fashion. When this happens, safety becomes an unconditional and unchallengeable value, showing insensitivity to individual autonomy and producing the kind of protectionist practice that until recently supported drastic overuse of physical and chemical restraints (Evans & Strumpf, 1989).

In addition to the argument from autonomy, the position taken by the Director of Nursing can be challenged by a "reverse" argument from equity and justice. If Miss Green is not allowed to smoke unattended while sighted residents are allowed to do so, it must be demonstrated that she presents a risk they do not present. Otherwise, she is not being treated equally but is the object of stereotypic judgment based on her disability.

In the actual resolution of this case the social worker and one of the home's administrators carefully observed Miss Green smoking and determined that she was not a safety risk. Both of these staff members then documented their advocacy for Miss Green on her chart, thus easing the Nursing Director's fears and sharing responsibility with her. The social worker also agreed to keep a close eye on Miss Green, reminding her of the hazards of smoking and her personal responsibility for safety.

This whole negotiating process might seem an elaborate maneuver around a relatively routine disagreement—especially when health care ethics is struggling with decisions about the removal of feeding tubes and other "edge of life" questions. But long-term care frequently revolves around seemingly small issues that in their cumulative, constant force shape the very quality of life for the elderly. Thus, the ethical terrain is often built of issues such as the freedom to smoke, to depart from the daily schedule, to choose one's roommates and tablemates, to have free and easy access to the telephone, to control the radio and television, etc. (Kane & Caplan, 1990).

In responding to these daily life issues, beneficent caregivers can exhibit all sorts of unreflective, well-intentioned paternalism. (The Nursing Director's postscript comment to Miss Green—reminding her that smoking is not good for her health—is a sharp example of this.) It is crucial, then, that the ethical implications of seemingly small freedoms and restrictions receive careful attention. Documenting a right to smoke is not bureaucratic overkill when a nursing home resident's daily life is subject to so many other limits and restrictions.

Case V

Mr. Fiske, a nursing home resident, is a diabetic who has recently developed a gangrenous foot. He is considered fully competent and he has, for the past ten days, steadfastly refused the surgical amputation recommended by the Medical Director of the nursing home as well as by another physician.

Instead, Mr. Fiske wants to receive treatment from a nutritional/vitamin specialist, not a physician, who is treating a friend of his suffering from cancer. The medical staff is convinced that the "specialist" is a quack, and they initially dismiss the request. Mr. Fiske then approaches a social worker whom he knows and asks for assistance. He has no family or friends to help him make the 50-mile trip to the nutritionist and he asks the social worker to arrange transportation for him.

The social worker has misgivings. But she has known Mr. Fiske for two years, and she feels that, on balance, supporting his course of action would be more beneficent than rebuffing it. In a case conference she argues that Mr. Fiske is liable to become more firmly entrenched in his refusal of amputation if this alternative option is refused. She suggests that his pursuit of vitamin therapy may be, at least in part, an attempt to assert control over his care.

The professionals caring for Mr. Fiske have an understandable desire to protect him from the negative consequences of his own bad judgment—as they see it. While care providers recognize the autonomous right of a mentally competent patient to refuse medical treatment, they may well hesitate to aid and abet what they consider to be futile treatment. Self-determination cannot command uncritical support when it works grievous harm and simultaneously pursues seemingly unreasonable forms of care.

The potentially life-threatening harm resulting from Mr. Fiske's refusal requires clear and convincing evidence of his mental capacity and informed consent (Drane, 1985). The case suggests that both these requirements have been met. But while respect for his autonomy would argue against a forced amputation, it does not rule out further exploration of his decision. Fuller understanding of Mr. Fiske's reasoning would, in fact, provide guidance for the staff in the grim prospects that might lie ahead.

It would be crucial then to examine the authenticity of Mr. Fiske's request (Collopy, 1988). Is his decision to pursue an alternate treatment in keeping with his past history and choices? Is it a sign that he is not choosing to die but only choosing to avoid amputation? How does he see the course of his condition, particularly if his visit to the nutritionist proves unavailing? More broadly, what are his attitudes toward traditional and alternative medicine, aggressive and palliative care, dependence and independence, the meaning of amputation and disability? How does he view his own dying and terminal care?

As suggested earlier in this article, a values history might prove helpful in charting what may be a difficult future for all involved in his care. Indeed, such a history might have forewarned his caregivers about the present problem. Even now, cooperation and conversation about his nutritional approach may provide an avenue for reconsidering his earlier refusal. It may help staff stay focused on what Mr. Fiske really wants, and perhaps keep them from divisive arguments based on their perceptions of what is right for him.

To the extent that Mr. Fiske's refusal of surgery is authentic, in keeping with the values and choices of his past life, the social workers advocacy for him is ethically sensible and sensitive. Rejecting his request to see the nutritionist might simply set off further non-cooperation from him, while an affirmation of his autonomy may in fact ease the current standoff. At the very least, the trip to the nutritionist may keep Mr. Fiske involved in a continuing conversation with his caregivers in the nursing home.

In the long run, the moral ambiguity of this case is instructive. The two extremes—amputating Mr. Fiske's foot without his consent or simply standing back and allowing his condition to worsen—create moral perplexity, a deep unease about choosing *either* beneficence *or* autonomy as a single guiding principle. The resulting disquiet suggests that Mr. Fiske's care providers should continue to "lathe" the case, pursuing communication, building trust, shaping their response to his view of the situation. Thus, his request to see the nutritionist should not be dismissed as a request for "futile treatment"—a request with little merit in the eyes of medical practitioners (not to mention the reimbursement system). Supporting Mr. Fiske's idiosyncratic request may strengthen the caregiving relationship for whatever lies ahead. It may also provide some important breathing space for beneficence, give care providers additional time and credibility to urge Mr. Fiske to accept surgery—or to come to terms themselves with his refusal.

CONCLUSION

These five cases offer a limited look at the kinds of ethical problems that can arise for social workers in long–term-care settings. We hope that even this cursory view indicates the need for interdisciplinary discussion between social workers and ethicists in health care.

For the future, that discussion could profitably pursue the following tasks: identifying the ethical dilemmas that are most frequent and most intractable in social work practice within long-term care; exploring the ethical principles and value commitments that are challenged by these dilemmas; examining the impact of regulation and reimbursement on social work ethics; developing a body of case material and commentary that will provide links between ethical theory and long–term-care practice; creating models for ethics committees, ethics consultations, and ethics case-conferences in long-term care; shaping programs to inform clients and their families of their rights within a *participatorial* framework rather than one that reduces long-term care to an adversarial provider–consumer encounter.

The dialogue between social work and bioethics may still be in its early stages, but even this brief agenda of issues indicates how expansive that dialogue could be.

NOTE

1. We are indebted to the following social workers who contributed reflections and case material from their own experience: Shulamis Charlop, Cynthia Greenberg, Irene Gutheil, Alice Hand, and Gary Lovitt.

REFERENCES

Blenkner, M. (1965). Social work and family relationships in later life with some thoughts on filial maturity. In E. Shanas & G. Streib (Eds.), *Social structure and the family* (pp. 46–59). Englewood Cliffs, NJ: Prentice-Hall.

Breckman, R., & Adelman, R. (1988). *Strategies for helping victims of elder mistreatment.* Newbury Park, CA: Sage.

Cohen, C. B. (Ed.). (1988). *Casebook on the termination of life-sustaining treatment and the care of the dying.* Bloomington: Indiana University Press, 1988.

Colby, W. H., Busalacchi, P., Baron, C., Robertson, J. A., Cranford, R. E., Lynn, J., & Glover, J. (1990). Cruzan: Clear and convincing? *Hastings Center Report, 20,* 5–11.

Coleman, N., & Dooley, J. (1990). Making the guardianship system work. *Generations, 14*(Suppl.), 47–50.

Collopy, B. (1988). Autonomy in long term care: Some crucial distinctions. *The Gerontologist, 28*(Suppl.), 10–17.

Collopy, B. (1992). *The use of restraints in long-term care: The ethical issues.* Washington, DC: American Association of Homes for the Aging.

Collopy, B., Dubler, N., & Zuckerman, C. (1990). The ethics of home care: Autonomy and accommodation. *Hastings Center Report, 20*(Suppl.), 1–16.

Conrad, A. P. (1989). Developing an ethics review process in a social service agency. *Social Thought, 15,* 102–115.

Cranford, R. E., Rie, M. A., Ackerman, F., & Callahan, D. (1991). Helga Wanglie's ventilator. *Hastings Center Report, 21,* 23–35.

Drane, J. F. (1985). The many faces of competency. *Hastings Center Report, 15,* 17–21.

Evans, L. K., & Strumpf, N. E. (1989). Tying down the elderly: A review of the literature on physical restraint. *Journal of the American Geriatrics Society, 37,* 132–136.

Generations. (1990). Autonomy and long-term care practice. *14*(Suppl.), 1–96.

The Gerontologist. (1988). Autonomy and long term care. *28*(Suppl.), 1–96.

Gibson, J. M. (1990). National values history project. *Generations 14*(Suppl.), 51–64.

Goffman, E. (1961). *Asylums.* Garden City, NY: Doubleday.

The Hastings Center (1989). *Guidelines on the termination of life-*

sustaining treatment and the care of the dying. Bloomington: Indiana University Press.

Iris, M. A. (l988). Guardianship and the elderly: A multi-perspective view of the decisionmaking process. *The Gerontologist, 28*(Suppl.), 39–45.

Iris, M. A. (1990). Threats to autonomy in guardianship decision making. *Generations, 14*(Suppl.), 39–41.

Johnson, C. L., & Grant, L. A. (1985). *The nursing home in American society.* Baltimore: The Johns Hopkins University Press.

Kane, R. A., & Caplan, A. L. (1990). *Everyday ethics: Resolving dilemmas in nursing home life.* New York: Springer.

Kayser-Jones, J. (1990). The use of nasogastric feeding tubes in nursing homes: Patient, family and health care provider perspectives. *The Gerontologist, 30*, 469–479.

Lidz, C. W., & Arnold, R. M. (1990). Institutional constraints on autonomy. *Generations, 14*(Suppl.), 65–68.

Loewenberg, F., & Dolgoff, R. (1988). *Ethical decisions for social work practice* (3rd ed.). Itasca, IL: Peacock.

Lynn, J. (Ed.) (1986). *By no extraordinary means: The choice to forego life-sustaining food and water.* Bloomington: Indiana University Press.

McCullough, L. (1984). Medical care of elderly patients with diminished competence: An ethical analysis. *Journal of the American Geriatrics Society, 32*, 150–153.

Moody, H. R. (1988). From informed consent to negotiated consent. *The Gerontologist, 28*(Suppl.), 64–70.

President's Commission for the Study of Ethical Problems in Medicine and Biomedical and Behavioral Research. (1982). Who is incapacitated and how is it to be determined? In *Making health care decisions* (pp. 169–175). Washington, DC: U.S. Government Printing Office.

President's Commission for the Study of Ethical Problems in Medicine and Biomedical and Behavioral Research. (1983). *Deciding to forego life-sustaining treatment: Ethical, medical, and legal issues in treatment decisions.* Washington, DC: U.S. Government Printing Office.

Reamer, F. G. (1982). *Ethical dilemmas in social work service.* New York: Columbia University Press

Scofield, G. R. (1991). Artificial feeding: The least restrictive alternative? *Journal of the American Geriatrics Society, 39*, 1217–1220.

Tancredi, L. R. (1987). The mental status examination. *Generations, 11*, 24–31.

Wasser, E. (1966) *Creative approaches in casework with the aging.* New York: Family Service Association of America.

Zuckerman, C. (1990). Home care clients and attendants: An uncertain relationship. In C. Zuckerman, N. N. Dubler, & B. Collopy (Eds.), *Home health care options* (pp. 183–196). New York: Plenum.

7

Interdisciplinary Teams in Geriatric Settings

Eileen R. Chichin and Ilse R. Leeser

THIS CHAPTER WILL PRESENT an overview of the current status of interdisciplinary teams, defining these teams, who their members are, where they are located, how they function, and the obstacles to their success. In addition, it will describe in detail three models of interdisciplinary teams, two community-based; the third, in a long–term-care institution. Finally, it will discuss the research and education needs of interdisciplinary teams and suggest where these teams will be in the future.[1]

BACKGROUND

Human beings are remarkably diverse and complex. And with increasing age they become markedly more so. As a result, old people as a group are more heterogenous than any other age group. To quote John W. Rowe, M.D., the president of Mount Sinai Medical Center in New York City and past president of the Gerontological Society of America, "If you know one old person, you know one old person" (1990).

As a result of their diversity and complexity, individuals in their later years have a constellation of needs that are manifested differently from those of their younger counterparts. Although persons of all ages have the same basic human needs, the characteristics of those needs are somewhat different with increasing age. The plethora of age-related physical changes, both normal and pathological, can test the mettle of the strongest among us. Compounding these are often drastic changes in the size and composition of one's social support network as a result of the death of age peers and even younger family members and friends. With retirement comes the loss of role and the loss of income. Additionally, and perhaps of equal importance, are the emotional reactions to these physical changes and social and financial losses. Thus, although from birth to death we all have needs for health care and social and emotional support, the needs of older persons are different and, in most cases, greater than those of the young. How, then, are we to meet those needs?

Most older people, even those with diminishing social networks, have adequate support systems. In addition, the health care needs of the vast majority of older persons are sufficiently met by a primary care physician. However, many diseases of the elderly are much less related to the aging process than to the loneliness, isolation, and frustration that come from separation from the mainstream of life and the loss of social status. A large proportion of the chronic diseases that affect our elderly population—arthritis, diabetes mellitus, chronic obstructive pulmonary disease (COPD), and cardiovascular diseases—could be prevented and/or successfully treated if our health care delivery systems were more fully and properly focused on the elderly (Dychtwald, 1986). For the minority of elderly individuals whose needs have reached a high degree of complexity, the answer may well be the interdisciplinary health care team.

What Is an Interdisciplinary Team?

Ducanis and Golin in their oft-quoted book *The interdisciplinary health care team* define such a team as "a functioning unit, composed of individuals with varied and specialized training, who coordinate their activities to provide services to a client or group of clients" (1979, p. 5). The terms "unit" and "coordinate" are key to this definition, and serve to distinguish interprofessional functioning from a multi-professional approach, characterized by "members of diverse disciplines . . . more or less informally interacting with—or tolerating—each other" (Bloom & Parad, 1976, p. 676).

Interdisciplinary teams have been used for many years in acute care settings. Such smoothly functioning groups as cardiac arrest teams in hospitals are an excellent example. Physicians, residents, interns, nurses, and respiratory therapists working together in these life-and-death situations are the classic interdisciplinary team, and have been dramatized extensively by the media. These teams often work no less effectively in real life situations.

Nor are interdisciplinary teams foreign to chronic care environments. Long–term-care facilities whose primary emphases are rehabilitative or supportive have long functioned effectively by utilizing members of diverse professions who as a group pooled their expertise to achieve maximum results for their patients. The success of these teams is dependent to a marked degree on the extent to which each member has a clearly defined role, and each discipline is recognized for its contributions. Smooth functioning is the result of mutual respect for one another's opinions and expertise. Although the presence of these factors do not necessarily guarantee the success of a team, their absence will most likely doom it to failure.

WHO ARE ITS MEMBERS?

A wide variety of individuals may participate in an interdisciplinary team. Teams may be as small as two persons, provided that at least one member is a professional (Ducanis & Golin, 1979). At a minimum, teams generally consist of a doctor, a nurse, and a social worker, or a psychologist and a social worker. Many teams, however, have many more participants and represent numerous disciplines, and, on occasion, may include a client and/or family members.

Very often, teams are composed of whoever is available. In those situations, when the need arises, consultants may be called in, or team members may be trained in other skills (Tsukuda, 1990). Schmitt, Farrell, and Heinemann (1988), in their review of research on interdisciplinary teams, cite some studies of teams consisting of a physician, a nurse, and a dietician, or a physician, nurse, and social worker. They found somewhat larger teams, however, to be more typical. Potential members include physicians (often a geriatrician), geriatric fellows, residents, rehabilitation nurses, discharge planning nurses, public health nurses, medical and psychiatric social workers, physical therapists, occupational therapists, pharmacists, dieticians, speech therapists, chaplains, physiatrists, recreation therapists, audiology therapists, geriatric dentistry fellows, nursing assistants, and clerical support personnel. In less traditional health care settings (e.g., a hospice, a home, or a community mental health center), interdisciplinary teams may include home-care aides, homemakers, drivers, and volunteers (Tsukuda, 1990).

In some situations, as noted earlier, the client as well as the family may be considered part of the team. The interdisciplinary team of the future will, most likely, in many more instances, count the client among its membership. There is evidence of a trend toward client participation in the decision-making process, probably a result of a growing consumer movement and the public's increased awareness of health care and human services. Further, the rise in overall educational level will result in a population more at ease with involvement in health care decisions that had traditionally been left to the medical profession (Ducanis & Golin, 1979). Professionals will be challenged to effectively incorporate clients into their teams, recognizing that individual self-determination is a key issue. Also key, however, is that team members work together, utilizing the fewest number of individuals needed to accomplish goals in an efficient and adequate manner.

WHERE IS IT LOCATED?

The location of interdisciplinary teams is not limited to the hospital or the long–term-care facility; they may function in any setting in which health or social services are provided. Thus, although many hospitals and nursing homes have interdisciplinary teams, such teams are also found in other institutional settings and in the community. Included among these settings are rehabilitation facilities, community mental health centers, alcohol treatment centers, hospices, and the home, in addition to any other settings capable of providing services through the use of teams.

How Does It Function?

Interdisciplinary health care teams are not unlike living organisms. For teams to survive, they must be continually involved in their own "socio-emotional, maintenance-oriented, or self-renewing functions" (Billups, 1987, p. 147). Teams are thought to progress through stages typical of small group development, and it has been hypothesized that interdisciplinary teams, while primarily task-oriented, still have a degree of "non-instrumental, expressive interaction that seems to be indicative of . . . underlying emotional processes" (Farrell, Heinemann, & Schmitt, 1986, p. 145). Through the process of group "growth and development," team members learn to overcome obstacles to communication and to develop methods for group decision making (Bennis & Shepard, 1974). Along the way, teams must develop strategies for interpersonal interaction, for resolving conflict, and for sustaining themselves. One approach is the development of rituals to encourage the regular participation of members. Farrell and his colleagues (1986) recall instances in which nurses in interdisciplinary teams used the ritual of providing refreshments at meetings to lure physicians (the "Reluctant Candidates") to attend. Humor and joking are often another "self-renewing" mechanism. Tsukuda (1990), in likening interdisciplinary teams to machines, suggests that they require ongoing maintenance. She recommends regular meetings and periodic workshops or retreats as one method of accomplishing this.

While its survival techniques are vital to an interdisciplinary team, its primary purpose, as noted above, is the tasks it must accomplish. Foremost among the characteristics of an interdisciplinary team, then, are a task-orientation, a client-based focus (Ducanis & Golin, 1979), and clear goals. Of equal importance in a successful team is leadership and the ability to make decisions (Tsukuda, 1990).

The goals set by an interdisciplinary team must be dynamic and able to adapt to the changing conditions of the client and of the client's environment. Goals need regular review, evaluation, and redefinition (Tsukuda, 1990), and must be communicated to all members. Teams function best when communication is clear, and, although it may take place by phone or in writing (Ducanis & Golin, 1979), face-to-face interaction is most often the norm. Feedback from team members, both on a formal and on an informal basis, provides necessary information to participants. Effective team functioning necessitates some mechanism for systematic sharing and exchanging of information (Schmitt, Farrell, & Heinemann, 1988). Some typical methods of information exchange include written patient care plans, interdisciplinary progress notes, and oral presentations at meetings.

The issues of tasks and roles within a team cannot be taken lightly. Tsukuda (1990) emphasizes that a team functions best when its tasks are decided upon before determining who is to accomplish them and how they should be accomplished. She further cautions that overlapping roles and shared expertise lay the groundwork for potential "conflict, duplication of efforts, and difficulty in defining professional boundaries" (1990, p. 672).

Leadership is another key component of an interdisciplinary team. Any belief that a team can function without a leader is erroneous. However, team leadership can and does change. Further, leadership may be dual (Chafetz, West, & Ebbs, 1987). The individual who may be the designated leader with respect to the maintenance and self-renewing functions of the group is often different from the individual who assumes leadership for the accomplishment of a particular task. Leadership in interdisciplinary teams is dynamic;

indeed, teams may use "shifting leadership," depending upon the issue at hand and who can best address it. Clearly, the decisions made by a team should depend to a great degree upon the input of those who are closest to the source of the problem and are therefore most likely to have the relevant information (Tsukuda, 1990).

Obstacles to Team Success: People and Places

Nearly two decades ago, Kane stated ". . . the interprofessional team . . . is generally agreed to be the major vehicle for serving society in this complex technological era" (1975, p. 5). However, although interdisciplinary teams can be a valuable resource in meeting the needs of many older individuals, there are a number of obstacles—both individual and organizational—that may hamper their successful functioning.

On the individual level, a number of issues come into play. Specifically, they fall into the areas of personality, power struggles, and allegiance to one's discipline (Fry & Miller, 1974; Tsukuda, 1990). In addition, role ambiguity, role conflict, and role overload are not uncommon (Billups, 1987; Farrell, Heinemann & Schmitt, 1986).

Incompatible personalities may wreak havoc in many settings. In an environment in which several individuals are expected to function as a team and to accomplish set goals, personalities that are in conflict not only hamper the achievement of the goals, but may also result in the internal destruction of the team. Power struggles affect both team process and team outcomes. More often than not, in teams that have physicians as members, the physician either is the designated leader or is perceived to be the leader. Issues of power in these situations are often a function of society's traditional awe of the medical profession, alone or in concert with the physician's socialization and assumptions of autonomy.

Intra-team conflict and communication problems may occur when team members function primarily in a discipline-specific manner rather than as team members. When theoretical perspectives and values differ, conflict is often the result (Sands, Stafford, & McClelland, 1990). For example, Mizrahi and Abramson (1985), in comparing physicians and social workers, focus on the issue of "the self" and relationships. Physicians, as part of their training, they state, are made to feel that their needs and "suffering" are inconsequential. In contrast, social work training emphasizes issues related to oneself and one's interpersonal relationships. Medicine emphasizes the individual over the environment, while social work views the person within the context of the environment and society. Clearly, members of these two professions, when working as a team, must be able to transcend their differences in values and orientation if the team is to function successfully. Optimal functioning is only possible when a team has a value base common to all members, a common language, and a conceptual framework that is understood by every participant (Abramson, 1984; Billups, 1987; Sands, Stafford, & McClelland, 1990).

The use of discipline-specific jargon may also prove problematical to team functioning. This can best be avoided by a definition of terms. For example, what exactly do we mean by social functioning? What is the definition of social supports (Kane, 1982)?

Role ambiguity and role conflict are potential problems and can have a deleterious effect on individual team members and also on the functioning of the team itself. These are most likely to occur when members of more than one discipline view the tasks to be performed as within their jurisdiction. Kulys and Davis (1987) describe such a situation in the hospice setting. In seeking to determine the extent to which nurses and social workers are "rivals in the provision of social services" (p. 101), the authors express the legitimate concern that, as nurses become more involved in psychosocial issues, they will usurp territory traditionally presumed to be that of the social worker. The failure of team members to work out their differences around these issues can place the client at a great disadvantage.

In the organizational area, the environment in which the

group exists has serious implications for its functioning and development (Farrell, Schmitt, & Heinemann, 1988). Often difficulties may arise as a result of the manner in which a team interacts with the overall system in which it functions (Tsukuda, 1990). This is perhaps most evident in institutional health care settings, which are hierarchical in nature. In these settings, power is concentrated at the top, and communicated downward. In contrast, power in interdisciplinary teams is somewhat more diffused and equalized among its members (Chafetz, West, & Ebbs, 1987). Often the ability of a team to function may be somewhat strained in a such a setting, that is, the interdisciplinary team attempts to survive as a "democracy" within the bounds of a bureaucracy (a hospital or nursing home).

Occasionally, the organizational constraints of the environment in which a team functions cause difficulties for the team. Farrell and his colleagues (1988) cite, for example, the rule requiring residents in teaching hospitals and nursing homes to rotate from service to service. A resident may be intimately involved in the team process when suddenly the time comes for rotation to another area of the facility. This forced departure has implications not only for the team process but, depending upon the level of involvement of the resident, may also affect the task at hand.

While organizational constraints in its immediate environment can impact upon the functioning of a team, more distant factors in its extended environment may also come into play. Included here are the effects of state and national policies, for example, that may dictate how services can be delivered or the manner in which they are reimbursed (Billups, 1987).

A COMMUNITY-BASED INTERDISCIPLINARY TEAM IN ACTION:
THE SOUTHEAST SENIOR CENTER FOR INDEPENDENT LIVING

Background

Availability of comprehensive health care to the aged population is frequently limited because of financial constraints and a societal orientation that emphasizes treatment over prevention. Most health plans—and especially Medicare—do not cover the cost of preventive measures. Many elderly clients are seen by a physician for the treatment of episodic or chronic illnesses, and health promotion and disease prevention are not given priority during these visits. Hospital clinics are frequently overcrowded, and here, too, only acute episodic care is provided. These factors serve to further intensify the problem, since elderly persons, more than any other segment of the population, need a great deal of time and attention, especially when it relates to advice and counseling regarding their health and optimal functioning.

Inadequacies in our system of delivering and financing health care are even more glaring when we recognize that health promotion and health maintenance activities are less expensive than treatment of illness (Nortman, 1988). Lubben, Weiler, and Chi (1989), in studying Medicaid elderly in California, found beneficial results when health promotion and treatment programs were geared specifically to this population. Further, the savings can be substantial when comprehensive senior centers are used to provide health care. The reduction of institutionalization and the use of Medicare and Medicaid, coupled with reduced usage of other public and private social service programs, were found to save two to three dollars for every dollar spent toward elder health care.

The following is a description of a program currently in existence which incorporates a health promotion program whose services are provided by an interdisciplinary team consisting of nurses, social workers, an independent living counselor, and a volunteer coordinator. The staff of this county-administered, federally funded center in Englewood, New Jersey attributes the success of its program to its focus on health promotion and the smooth interaction of its interdisciplinary health care team.

The Center Today

The Southeast Center for Independent Living opened in the late 1970s to serve eleven towns in Bergen County, New

Jersey. An innovative center for senior citizens, its philosophy focuses on keeping senior citizens out of institutions by promoting their physical, mental, and emotional health. Further, it attempts to keep its clients socially active and financially independent and works to change their lifestyles from passive to active. Its comprehensive services include a health care program designed to promote and maintain optimum health for the elderly. Among its many services are individual and group counseling geared toward problems facing older people (i.e., loneliness, isolation, loss, and grief), educational and recreational programs, exercise and nutrition programs, and dental, optometry, and podiatry services. When needed, transportation to and from the center is provided.

The only eligibility requirements are age (60 years or over) and residence in one of the eleven towns that the catchment area comprises. Accordingly, any older person—well or frail—who resides in the catchment area is welcome to utilize the services of the Center.

The Center offers a unique and innovative interdisciplinary approach to meeting individual needs. Every client who registers at the center undergoes a complete needs assessment, after which an interdisciplinary plan is designed and implemented. If necessary, referrals are made to other resources in the community, such as long-term in-depth counseling, financial aid, housing, legal services, volunteer work or part-time employment, Social Security, and Medicaid and Medicare.

The core of the service delivery is the nursing and the social work staffs. Nurse practitioners and social workers work together closely to meet the physical, social, and emotional needs of the elderly clients. The nurse practitioner regularly refers clients to the social worker for the evaluation of problems requiring social work expertise, and the social worker makes regular referrals to the nurse as needed. A routine part of the functioning of the Center incorporates a smooth flow of communication between nursing and social work staffs. As a result, the population served by the Center realizes that all their problems and concerns are taken into consideration, and taken seriously, and that every attempt is made to address individual concerns speedily and successfully.

The nurse practitioner's role in this Center is primarily one of health maintenance, health promotion, and disease prevention. After a complete health care evaluation has been performed, the client is advised how to follow a health care regimen that will improve and maintain optimal physical and emotional health. For example, female clients are advised, among other things, to have annual mammography and are taught breast self-examination. Male clients are taught testicular self-examination. Clients are counseled regarding wholesome nutrition, adequate physical exercise, and other measures they must take to ensure good health.

The nurse may identify health care problems, possibly resulting from poor nutrition, lack of physical exercise, lack of support systems, and poor housing or environmental conditions. When necessary, clients are counseled to consult their physicians, and copies of all laboratory results are forwarded to the appropriate physician. Frequently the nurse practitioner will directly contact the physician, and the physician in turn will provide feedback to the nurse practitioner after seeing the client.

The social worker works closely with the client to meet a wide variety of other needs, with respect both to basic services and in the emotional area. Social workers are responsible for such instrumental requirements as financial support and transportation to nutrition centers in the community. Equally important is their role in assisting clients to mobilize their own support systems through better communication with friends and family.

Old age is characterized, in most cases, by a continuum of losses. The social worker assists clients to adjust to loss and helps them work through the grief process. Issues of social isolation are also addressed, and clients are taught ways of adapting to this difficult concomitant of the later years. The need for a change in lifestyle, especially after retirement, when faced with chronic illness, or when one loses a loved one, is also a problem that falls into the social worker's domain.

In monthly case conferences, all nursing and social work team members discuss the various aspects of case management. All efforts are geared to ensuring that clients are seen by members of the professional team representing nursing and social work so that all the needs of the clients are met adequately and successfully.

The goals for each client at the Southeast Senior Center for Independent Living include optimum physical, emotional, and social functioning. However, each client's goals are individualized, and the tasks required to meet those goals are carried out by the appropriate member of the interdisciplinary team. Task assignment takes into consideration the nature of the task to be performed and the respective discipline and abilities of the team member who will carry it out. The clear defining of the roles of each team member and the careful assignment of tasks results in the most effective solutions to client problems with minimum stress on the team members. This Center is one model of an interdisciplinary team, illustrative of an effective approach to meeting the complex needs of older persons.

AN INTERDISCIPLINARY TEAM IN A
LONG-TERM CARE INSTITUTION:
THE JEWISH HOME AND HOSPITAL FOR AGED

The Jewish Home and Hospital for Aged (JHHA) in New York City is a teaching nursing home whose three inpatient long–term-care facilities and a short-term inpatient rehabilitation unit serve approximately 1500 residents on a daily basis. Also under its auspices are a number of community-based services, including adult day-care centers for the frail elderly and Alzheimer's patients, a geriatric day center for the blind and the visually impaired, a long-term home health care program, a geriatric outreach program, and an Alzheimer's disease at-home emergency respite program, in addition to residential housing facilities for both well and frail elderly.

Throughout the Home and its many programs are numerous interdisciplinary teams.

The interdisciplinary team on each of JHHA's nursing units holds a weekly team meeting that brings together a number of individuals representing many disciplines. Among them are geriatric medicine and geriatric nursing— the former represented by an internist and a psychiatrist; the latter, by a head nurse, a staff nurse, a rehabilitation nurse, and a staff development instructor. In addition, present at the meeting are a pharmacist, a dietician, a social worker, a physical therapist, and a staff member from therapeutic recreation. On the short-term rehabilitation unit, team members also include a physiatrist. And, on the teaching unit, additional team members include a geriatric fellow, a geriatric nurse practitioner, and possibly a medical student. Occasionally, family members are in attendance, and when the resident is able, he or she may attend.

The typical one-hour meeting usually focuses on two or three residents. In the course of the meeting, the team uses a comprehensive nursing assessment to guide the development of treatment plans for residents. Led by the head nurse, the patient's overall plan of care is reviewed, focusing particularly on short- and long-term goals and incorporating both physical and psychosocial needs. Discussion ranges from topics as basic as eating (which, in the nursing home, may be fraught with complexity) to as perplexing as the issue of "Do Not Resuscitate" (DNR), which, of course, is made with input from the resident or family. Opinions are sought from all team members, with special emphasis on the skills of those members which are most relevant to a resident's particular problems.

Of greatest benefit to the resident is the review of his or her current status and the current treatment plan; possible alternatives are evaluated as well. Team interaction is vital to this process, and only when some degree of consensus among team members is reached is a decision finalized and the task to be accomplished assigned to the appropriate team member.

What is perhaps most evident in observing the functioning

of this team in a long–term-care setting is the importance of an interdisciplinary approach for individuals with such complex needs. For example, a nurse may make note of a resident who exhibits behavioral problems. Input is received at the meeting from the psychiatrist, who believes the problems may be psychiatric in etiology, and the pharmacist, who suggests they may be the side effect of a medication. Or, in determining the need to discuss a DNR order with the family of a cognitively impaired resident, the team judges which particular member has the closest relationship with the family.

Clearly, long–term-care facilities are optimum settings for interdisciplinary teams. Most long–term-care settings house the frailest and most dependent individuals in our society. Interdisciplinary teams are the obvious approach to meeting the complex needs of this population, and, when effective, can do much toward restoring or maintaining dignity and a maximum level of independence.

INTERDISCIPLINARY TEAMS IN COMMUNITY MENTAL HEALTH: THE OUTPATIENT MENTAL HEALTH SERVICE AT HACKENSACK MEDICAL CENTER

Traditionally, older people have been reluctant to utilize the services of mental health professionals, preferring instead to turn to their primary care physicians. However, a community mental health program that uses a team approach may be more acceptable to older people. Further, it can also serve the needs of their families. One such program is the Geriatric Evaluation Service at the Outpatient Mental Health Service at Hackensack Medical Center in Hackensack, New Jersey.

The Team and the Process

The Geriatric Evaluation Service is designed to evaluate a variety of psychiatric conditions manifested by older persons. Accordingly, this program typically sees patients suffering from dementia. More often than not, individuals who exhibit symptoms of dementing illness (and their families) seek the services of a neurologist. However, the philosophy of this program is that patients and families are better served by the ongoing communication and coordination of the respective professionals on the team than if they were to consult each discipline individually. Through the use of an interdisciplinary team, the Geriatric Evaluation Service assesses the individual patient and works with the patient's family to plan a course of care.

Prospective patients are referred to the Geriatric Evaluation Service through a variety of sources, including the Office for the Aging, the Alzheimer's Association, adult daycare centers and family support groups. In addition, word-of-mouth and the program's brochure also result in referrals to the program. Interestingly, although the hospital of which this Outpatient Mental Health Service is a part has grown to be a relatively large medical center, it remains, for many older persons, their community hospital. Accordingly, when they have a health-related problem, they call the hospital, and may ultimately be referred to the Geriatric Evaluation Service. This program has no catchment area, but most of its patients or their families reside in the county. Health insurance, Medicare, and Medicaid are the usual methods of reimbursement.

The interdisciplinary team in the Geriatric Evaluation Service consists of a psychiatrist, a geriatric mental health specialist who is an MSW, and a consulting neurologist. The first point of contact for all patients and families seeking the services of this program is the geriatric mental health specialist who speaks to the inquiring individual by telephone. At that time, the situation is assessed, and if appropriate, an appointment is scheduled for the patient and the family. Before starting the mental health evaluation, the patient is instructed to contact his or her private physician to have a physical examination that includes additional blood tests which will rule out reversible dementias. (If the prospective patient has no private physician, the name of a cooperating doctor will be suggested.)

The first meeting with the patient and family is scheduled

with the geriatric mental health specialist. At this time, a history is taken, and the family, who participates in all interviews, is asked to fill out a questionnaire describing the patient's behavior. A mental status test specially designed for the elderly is administered. The family is asked how they have been coping with the situation to date, and the extent of any care arrangements. Also at this time, the geriatric specialist may recommend some programs to the family. Possible suggestions to aid family caregivers include support groups and adult day care. Families may also be instructed regarding legal and financial procedures, and the need to make an application to Medicaid. Finally, the geriatric specialist writes a report of her assessment for the psychiatrist, and an appointment is made for the patient and family to be seen by the chief psychiatrist.

The meeting with patient, family, and the psychiatrist is the second step in the process. Because mental status can vary from day to day, the psychiatrist does another mental status exam. She also talks to the family about their observations. Often, at this time, if there is evidence of depression, agitation, or other psychiatric symptoms, the psychiatrist may decide to prescribe medication.

The patient is then seen by the third member of the interdisciplinary team, the neurologist, who has received written reports from both the geriatric mental health specialist and the psychiatrist. The neurologist conducts a thorough evaluation of the patient, including an EEG and usually either a CT scan or an MRI. In addition, he administers yet another mental status exam. At the conclusion of his evaluation, the neurologist sends a written report of his findings to the geriatric mental health specialist and also to the patient's primary care physician.

The final step in the evaluation process involves reporting the findings to the family and, where appropriate, the patient. Most often, a diagnosis of dementia confirms suspicions the family may have had for some time.

Since the purpose of the geriatric evaluation service *is* evaluation, its task is complete at this time. The role of the interdisciplinary team concludes by directing the family toward the resources necessary to cope with dementing illness.

The members of the interdisciplinary team in the Geriatric Evaluation Service have clearly defined and closely intertwined roles. While each is involved in the assessment process to varying degrees, each assessment is from a different perspective. Planning and implementing treatment are done in collaboration, while referrals to appropriate resources are usually done by the geriatric mental health specialist. Communication takes place on a regular basis, via written reports, telephone conversations, and face-to-face meetings. Written reports and follow-up phone calls are the usual methods of interaction between the neurologist and the other team members, while the geriatric mental health specialist and the chief psychiatrist meet face to face. These meetings take place on a weekly basis to discuss cases and their disposition, and more often if a crisis arises. Respect for one another's roles and abilities is thought to keep this team functioning at a high level and serving its patients and their families in an optimal fashion.

CURRENT NEEDS IN THE AREA OF INTERDISCIPLINARY TEAMS

Interdisciplinary teams appear to be alive and well, and have the potential for growth in the future. However, in order to continue, especially in an era of cost constraints, we must increase our efforts to document their value and ensure that they are used in an effective and efficient manner. Two of the most effective means of achieving this are research and education.

Research in the area of interdisciplinary teams is in its embryonic stages as far as methodology is concerned. Schmitt, Farrell and Heinemann (1988), in their review of current research in the field, found numerous problems. They suggest that interdisciplinary team research is fraught with difficulties in the area of design, construct validity, the populations studied, and outcomes. Team research has been further criticized for its reliance on case study formats

(Stahelski & Tsukuda, 1990). These issues must be addressed in order to validate the need for and effectiveness of interdisciplinary teams in serving the needs of our older population.

Clearly, educational programs for interdisciplinary teams are also a necessity. Such programs can facilitate a team's ability to accomplish its goals. In addition, they can educate team members in team process and in the use of effective techniques for working with members of other disciplines.

Heinemann (1987–1988) describes two models of team education currently in use. The first, the Focused Team Analysis and Training (FTAT) Program (Farrell, Schmitt, Heinemann, Evans, & Patchett, 1985) is a team-specific educational program. It involves interviewing each team member and observing him or her over the course of a day. Videotapes of team interaction and educational feedback sessions are used over a period of several weeks. Participants evaluate the program both at its conclusion and again in six months to assess its long-term impact. This program, specially designed for a particular team, uses considerable educational resources over an extended period of time. However, it is believed to be the most effective in improving a team's ability to function. Obviously, time and cost are important factors to consider in the use of this type of educational program.

A second type of educational program currently in use is the preplanned workshop. Designed to run from a half-day to two days, workshops can provide an introduction and overview of the interdisciplinary team approach, or can focus on one specific aspect of teamwork. Often participants find this format useful, although the limitations of time result in a more superficial approach to the subject matter.

Although both these educational programs are effective, each has its limitations, especially with respect to numbers served, time issues, and the status of the participants. The team-specific approach can deal with only about 10 to 15 team members, while the workshop can educate from 20 to 80 persons at a time, but in a more limited fashion. Team-specific programs are "tailor-made" for a specific team and require several months for completion, while workshops are geared to a more general audience and rarely last longer than two days. Students may participate in workshops, but the team-specific model is rarely open to students, and, therefore, in this case students lose the opportunity to be exposed in depth early in their careers to this important model of service delivery. Heinemann (1987–1988) believes that the ideal educational format would incorporate both the team-specific and the workshop approaches. As a model, she cites the Veterans Administration's Interdisciplinary Team Training in Geriatric (ITTG) Program currently in use in 12 model VA medical centers. (See Heinemann, 1987–1988, for a detailed description of these programs.)

<h2 style="text-align:center">WHAT DOES THE FUTURE HOLD FOR INTERDISCIPLINARY TEAMS?</h2>

Given our increasing elderly population, and especially the concentration of the frailest individuals at the very end of the age continuum, creative methods of providing service are vital. We know that older persons as a group are the largest users of health care services, and health care costs for the elderly represent approximately one-third of the nation's health care expenditures (Stanhope & Lancaster, 1988). Thus, while soaring health care costs are a problem for all age groups, they are of particular concern for those 65 years of age and older, many of whom have at least one chronic health problem.

The interdisciplinary team model has shown evidence—at least informally—of being a promising and effective approach for those with multiple health care and social needs. Further, such a model might prove highly effective—both cost-wise and otherwise—if its focus incorporated prevention in addition to treatment. Clearly, we need some empirical research to document the effectiveness of the team approach, with respect both to humanitarian and to financial issues. And, of course, we must recognize that many older people receive adequate and appropriate care through a single, primary care provider, and that, in these cases, the use of interdisciplinary teams is unnecessary and inefficient (Tsukuda, 1990).

Nonetheless, there are other instances in which, most likely, interdisciplinary teams are the most appropriate solution. When a number of needs must be addressed simultaneously (e.g., physical, emotional, and financial) the team approach is often the optimum approach. In those situations, we must develop mechanisms to ensure that teams function at the highest possible level. Clearly, educational programs will play a major role in this endeavor, and mechanisms for regular evaluation must be built in.

Tsukuda (1990) reminds us of the heterogeneity and complexity of older persons, and the impact upon them of numerous psychological, emotional, and environmental factors. Clearly, the training and talents of many disciplines can best meet the needs of many older individuals. In light of the expected increase in size of our older population, it would be wise to anticipate the increased use of interdisciplinary teams in the future.

NOTE

1. Appreciation is expressed to Hennie Ostrower, M.S.W., A.C.S.W., for her assistance with this chapter.

REFERENCES

Abramson, M. (1984). Collective responsibility in interdisciplinary collaboration: An ethical perspective for social workers. *Social Work in Health Care, 10*(1), 35–43.

Billups, J. O. (1987) Interprofessional team process. *Theory into practice, 26*(2), 146–152.

Bennis, W. G., & Shepard, H. S. (1974). A theory of group development. In Gibbard, G. S., Hartman, J. J., & Mann, R. D. (Eds.), *Analysis of groups* (pp. 127–153). San Francisco: Jossey-Bass.

Bloom, B. L., & Parad, H. J. (1976). Interdisciplinary training and interdisciplinary functioning: A survey of attitudes and practice in community mental health. *American Journal of Orthopsychiatry, 46*, 669–677.

Butler, R. N., & Lewis, M. (1982). *Aging and mental health*. St. Louis: Mosby.

Carnevali, D., & Patrick, M. (1986). *Nursing management for the elderly* (2nd ed.). Philadelphia: Lippincott.

Chafetz, P., West, H., & Ebbs, E. (1987). Overcoming obstacles to cooperation in interdisciplinary long-term care teams. *Journal of Gerontological Social Work, 11*(3/4), 131–140.

Ducanis, A. J., & Golin, A. K. (1979). *The interdisciplinary health care team*. Germantown, MD: Aspen Systems Communication.

Dychtwald. K. (1986) *Wellness and health promotion for the elderly*. Rockville, MD: Aspen Systems Corporation.

Farrell, M. P., Heinemann, G. D., & Schmitt, M. H. (1986). Informal roles, rituals, and styles of humor in interdisciplinary health care teams: Their relationship to stages of group development. *International Journal of Small Group Research, 2*(2), 153–162.

Farrell, M. P., Schmitt, M. H., & Heinemann, G. D. (1988). Organizational environments of health care teams: Impact on team development and implications for consultations. *International Journal of Small Group Research, 4*(1), 31–53.

Farrell, M. P., Schmitt, M. H., Heinemann, G. D., Evans, P. L., & Patchett, C. (1985). Focused team analysis and training: Geriatric team development at a Veterans Administration medical center. *Proceedings from the Sixth Annual Team Conference: 1984*. Hartford, CT: University of Connecticut.

Fry, L., & Miller, J. P. (1974). The impact of interdisciplinary teams on organizational relationships. *Sociological Quarterly*, 15, 417–431.

Heinemann, G. D. (1987–1988). Education for interdisciplinary practice in geriatric health care settings. *AGH Exchange, 12*(2), 1–3.

Kane, R. A. (1975). *Interprofessional teamwork*. Manpower Monograph No. 8. Syracuse, NY: Syracuse University School of Social Work.

Kane, R. A. (1982). Lessons for social work from the medical model: A viewpoint for practice. *Social Work, 27*(4), 315–321.

Kemper, P., Applebaum, R., & Harrigan, M. (1987). Community care demonstrations: What have we learned? *Health Care Financing Review, 8*(4), 87–100.

Kulys, R., & Davis, M. A. (1987). Nurses and social workers: Rivals in the provision of social services? *Health and Social Work, 12*(2), 101–112.

Lubben, J., Weiler, P., & Chi, I. (1989). Health practices of the elderly poor. *American Journal of Public Health, 79*(6), 731–734.

Mizrahi, T., & Abramson, J. (1985). Sources of strain between physicians and social workers in health care settings. *Social Work in Health Care, 10*(3), 33–51.

Nortmann, P. (1988). Successful aging and quality of life in the modern technological era. Paper presented at the Eighth Annual Conference of the Northeast Gerontological Society, Bridgeport, CT.

Rowe, J. W. (1990). First Annual Beatrice Goldberg Lecture. New York: The Jewish Home and Hospital for Aged.

Sands, R. G., Stafford, J., & McClelland, M. (1990). "I beg to differ": Conflict in the interdisciplinary team. *Social Work in Health Care, 14*(3), 55–72.

Schmitt, M. H., Farrell, M. P., & Heinemann, G. D. (1988). Conceptual and methodological problems in studying the effects of interdisciplinary geriatric teams. *The Gerontologist, 28*(6), 753–764.

Stahelski, A. J., & Tsukuda, R. (1990). Predictors of cooperation in health care teams. *Small Group Research, 21*(2), 220–233.

Stanhope, M., & Lancaster, J. (1988). *Community health nursing.* St. Louis: Mosby.

Tsukuda, R. (1990). Interdisciplinary collaboration: Teamwork in geriatrics. In C. K. Cassel, D. E. Reisenberg, L. B. Sorenson, & J. R. Walsh (Eds.), *Geriatric medicine* (2nd ed.) (pp. 668–675). New York: Springer-Verlag.

8

Case Management: A Pivotal Service in Community-Based Long-Term Care

Sally Robinson

THE FOLLOWING DISCUSSION of case management is offered from a primarily experiential perspective—one that has been developed and tested during nearly 20 years of service planning and implementation in a municipal Office for the Aging. These services are delivered along a continuum of assistance ranging from the impersonal provision of information to intensive, protective interventions. Services along this continuum are themselves highly individuated so that each one may be more or less impersonal or intensive and protective. For example, information may be provided as part of a public awareness campaign to raise the consciousness of all age groups about age specific needs and problems, entitlements, and services. Or, such information may be offered as part of a case management response that seeks to develop and sustain the capability of a particular older person for life in the community.

Case management is a process of needs assessment, coordinated planning and arrangement for service, and monitoring of the social care assessed according to a plan agreed to by the client and the case manager. Case management itself may be more or less personal or intensive, depending upon the need to be addressed, the client's willingness and ability to help him- or herself, and the degree of his or her social isolation or involvement in a caring, competent informal support network.

THE SERVICE POPULATION

Although all persons 60 years of age and over are typically eligible for and are often recipients of assistance from Offices for the Aging, as well as from other programs and agencies whose services are age specific, the burgeoning of the 60-plus population has generated increasing and widespread attention to the definition and variability of need among older people. In fact, the relevance of old age to need is being questioned. Legislators who represent constituencies in competition with older people for scarce public health and welfare dollars are asking whether growing older is a valid, reliable, or, indeed, equitable indicator of need and concomitant right to public resources. The Older Americans Act and other legislation seeking to maximize the well-being of older people provide for the direction of service attention to those most in need, but preserve age as the basic and overriding eligibility standard for benefits thereunder. For example, in New York, the Older Americans Act and state funding guidelines target certain subsets of the aging population: low-income households, minorities, persons who live alone, persons 75 and older, persons with functional disabilities, and, most recently, women and veterans. The service assumption is that, although all persons 60 and older may be needy, these subsets of older adults are in greater need and should receive priority in service delivery, including case management. The practice reality is that, although most older persons who seek services directly or who are referred for help by concerned others belong to one or more of the targeted groups, older persons who do not belong to any of these groups also seek and demand assistance based on their age eligibility alone and, more important, based on their perception that age confers upon them a need for and right to public benefits.

Without engaging in a full discussion of the issue of age vis-à-vis need, it is important to introduce this issue as one that permeates and critically influences the effective delivery of case management services. The challenge and opportunity for case managers in this regard are first to recognize when the age vis-à-vis need factor pertains in case management decision making and then to confront it by avoiding the rote application of either age eligibility or targeting criteria. Each client's need should be carefully differentiated before service alternatives are explored. Only then should eligibility and qualification for one or more services be examined. Eligibility should be established first. Then, qualification in terms of targeting services should be done. Finally, it has to be determined whether or not the client can privately obtain the services that are essential to his or her well-being at home. Can the client pay for care or count on the support of family and friends? Although these distinctions as to qualification for services are particularly useful in the application of publicly subsidized resources, they are also pertinent in any context of limited ability to meet demand for care.

Client Self-Determination

An issue related to the issue of age vis-à-vis need is client self-determination as expressed in the client's service preferences. It is generally agreed that client autonomy, defined as an inherent or natural right to make informed treatment/service choices, is a basic social work principle. Especially in case management, the social worker's role of facilitating and enabling client choice is considered essential to an effective process of assistance. Ideally, the service choices available to clients capture their service preferences. Realistically, the choices available to clients often are not those they prefer or are willing to consider at all. In the fragmented service delivery system in which case managers attempt to support a client's self-determining choice, service eligibility and qualification criteria and rules may supersede client preference so that none of the choices available to the client are preferred ones.

For example, a client may be eligible for and prefer home-delivered meals. However, under targeting mandates and/or by reason of an alternatively available resource (most typically, a willing and able relative), the client may not qualify for this service. Other choices presented to him or her, such as ordering from a nearby restaurant or receiving transportation assistance to a congregate meals site, may be rejected on the basis of age eligibility for the home-delivered meals. The client may persistently advocate that age alone entitles him or her to home-delivered meals. The challenge to case managers in situations like this is to avoid a similarly doctrinaire response. Note that one is available: the home-delivered meals service is not a statutory entitlement. Unlike Medicaid, for example, eligibility and qualification for home-delivered meals do not ensure the client receipt of this service; they mean only that he or she is eligible to apply for the service. The important point here is not whether meals are a legal entitlement. Rather, the point is that the doctrinaire or dogmatic approach to meeting need—either by the client or by the case manager—will not ensure humane, effective use of resources to meet need.

The case manager's challenge is to provide a solution that meets the client's need without treating him or her as a case instead of as a person. Here is another example of a situation in which client preference is not easily served by available service choices. A client eligible and qualified for both home-delivered meals under the Older Americans Act and home-maker services under Medicaid may prefer home-delivered meals. However, accessible Medicaid-provided assistance by law supersedes client's preference. Under regulations governing the public provision of home-delivered meals, Medicaid home care is considered to be an overriding equivalent alternative. Of course, although a comparable service, Medicaid home care is not really an equivalent alternative because under the Medicaid program the client must pay for his or her own food. Further, the quality of the food provided may differ between the two programs. And, most important to many clients, the provision of meals under Medicaid requires the presence of a homemaker. The presence of the homemaker raises quality-of-care issues that are not involved in the simple delivery of a meal.

The challenge to case managers in this and similar cases

is not only to present the bureaucratic choice, which may not allow the client to decide his or her preference, but also to persist in working with the client to develop choices that do capture his or her preference and, thereby, are self-determining. In this example, further exploration with the client of his or her preference for home-delivered meals might uncover client concerns about preserving the privacy of her home in a small apartment. The client may fear that the homemaker's presence would be intrusive. The case manager would then have more information which could lead to the development of additional alternatives. For example, it might be suggested to the client that the homemaker could escort him or her to a congregate meals site where, in addition to the meal, the company of others could be enjoyed without impinging on client's privacy at home.

The point in these examples is that the enabling and promotion of client self-determination by case managers always requires, even in the most apparently routine cases, that client participation in the decisions affecting his or her life be sought and validated. Presumptions as to the client's perception of the service alternatives may actually limit the client's choices and, thereby, the expression of self-determination. Even when a client's judgment has been assessed as impaired due to physical or mental illness or developmental disability, the case management challenge remains one of nurturing and sustaining client self-determination to the utmost degree by ensuring a needs assessment and a care-planning process in which the client is encouraged to participate.

Practice experience reveals that every client, including persons who exhibit extreme mental disturbance and anguish, can participate productively when offered an opportunity to do so, even though their participation may consist only of their description of the hallucinations or delusions that plague them. It is not uncommon for case managers to be called upon to help older persons whose paranoia or other mental illness isolates them. These elders cannot make use of outpatient psychiatric treatment, which requires a willingness, typically precluded by their illness, to travel to the clinician. Nor is inpatient treatment an option, as it is predicated either on a willingness to be hospitalized or on the client's acute and imminent life-threatening expression of illness, the only basis for involuntary hospitalization. When case managers are called upon to intervene with clients whose mental illness, although not life-threatening, is associated with their isolation and inability to handle the demands of daily life at home, the client's input may be the only input available with which to begin the development of ameliorating service strategies. For these elderly, the lack of publicly funded at-home diagnostic and treatment services means that case managers in Offices for the Aging or other general service agencies are often not only the first, but also the last resort for the access of care.

These cases pose a real challenge to the training and supervision of case managers in non-medical settings. Perhaps the challenge of caring for these older people should belong to specialized health care providers. However, these providers typically do not address either the physical or the mental health needs of isolated elderly, who are resistant to leaving their homes for the services of these professionals. Training and supervision of case managers for work with these older people must, therefore, be directed toward learning techniques for accessing and appropriately consulting with physicians and other health care specialists who do not make house calls.

Case management's promotion of client self-determination is challenged when clients will not cooperate in their own behalf because of psychiatric disorders and cognitive deficits. Often, case managers are relied upon to make decisions regarding the client's ability to decide, decisions that are more properly made by health care specialists. Case managers must be trained to describe the client's behavior so that the physician or other mental health professional is able to give useful advice. Therefore, case managers should have an informed basis for observing client behavior as this may impact on self-determination.

Much has been written about patient and client autonomy, particularly in relation to decisions to accept or reject medical treatment. It is becoming more common for major health care institutions, both acute and long-term care, to employ ethicists to mediate when patients appear to be unable to decide for themselves. Various mechanisms, such as living wills, health care proxies, and involuntary protective service laws are used to help people who are or may become incapacitated in their decision making. The case manager in a nonspecialized setting must become conversant with the literature and should be trained specifically in the availability and application of these mechanisms.[1]

THE HELPING RELATIONSHIP

The client's self-determining participation in the case management process can be maximized by the case manager's conscious development of an alliance with the client. This positive emotional bonding affirms the personhood and self-worth of both client and case manager, and can powerfully enable the client's appropriate perception and use of available assistance.[2]

Assessment of need may take one or more client contacts. The case manager must move at the client's pace, working with the client to clarify his or her needs. The worker may identify the needs immediately, but must adjust to the client's pace to avoid pre-emptive actions. Some clients may be unable to participate fully in the assessment of need. However, this may be because the client simply is not as far along in the process as the worker. What may be a classic case situation to the case manager is often a painful and confusing situation for the client.

The importance of the helping relationship in moving clients toward problem solving and in enabling them to use help (Perlman, 1979) must not be overlooked. The relationship provides the supportive context for the case management process.

THE FUNCTION AND PURPOSE OF CASE MANAGEMENT

Case management's function is client-centered. It activates a coordinated community response to client need in order to develop and sustain the client's ability to manage at home without undue stress and risk. Case management's coordinative function positions this service as a pivotal intervention in a fragmented services environment, an intervention that treats the client as a whole person. But is it realistic to expect that such a coordinative function and integrative purpose can be implemented in a service structure which a leading gerontologist characterizes as one of specialization in which "the segmenting of service does not match the unity of a client's life" (Morris, 1989, p. 497)? According to Morris, the function of case management systems in the midst of proliferating specialties is unclear and confusing to both clients and staff. He suggests that the volume of unmet need may actually increase due to the complexity of services which are specialty-driven in terms of their "excluding rules to fit applicant to specialty" (1989, p. 497).

The challenge to case management is in sustaining professional accountability for client-centered service. Once the delivery of the service or entitlement itself becomes the primary concern, the case manager's accountability to the client is in danger of being displaced. The reader is reminded of the earlier discussion about the importance of assessing client need before dealing with issues of services eligibility and qualification. The clerical application of rules and regulations for the receipt of an entitlement or other benefit is not case management, although such tasks are often handled by case managers and may be so time-consuming and demanding that the definitive case management perspective is at risk of submersion in all the paperwork.

GAP-FILLING SERVICES

A client-centered perspective is conducive to the identification by the case manager of gaps in available services to meet clients' needs. These gaps may be in both formal and informal services. Common gaps in services are caused by: (1) limited provider capacity (not enough of a particular service, like home-delivered meals, to meet demand); (2)

relatively unusual or specialized nature of the need to be met (for example, a need for a homemaker who is bi-lingual in and/or conversant with an untypical language or culture); (3) access-problems like insufficient public transportation and no alternate travel means for home-care personnel; and (4) an absence of home-based psychiatric services. A common gap in clients' informal support system is the presence in the elder's home of an adult child who is unable and usually unwilling to provide care, but who influences his or her parent to decline help from formal sources or other family members.

Not only do these and other service gaps challenge the case manager's ability to seek and apply alternatives, albeit often not equivalent, to client need, but they also offer the case manager an opportunity to become involved in macro-level policy change. Successful advocacy for long–term-care policy initiatives depends upon the micro-level documentation of under-met or unmet need. In this regard, case managers have an obligation to apprise and work with agency administrators and boards and elected officials to identify and work toward relevant change.

The utility to the case manager of a collegial, coordinated services approach is perhaps most evident when there is a gap in needed assistance. A reliable intra- and inter-organizational professional support network can be of inestimable value to the efforts of case managers to handle service gaps.

CASE MANAGEMENT SETTINGS

Maintaining professional accountability for client-centered service may be complicated by conflicting organizational accountabilities. Professional performance that promotes collegial, collaborative working relationships with both clients and providers can contribute significantly to the development of client-centered service norms and models. However, this type of case management performance is dependent upon the degree of organizational support and facilitation available to the case manager. For example, the influence of provider settings and other external factors on care-planning decisions was studied in four HMOs. The findings suggest organizational differences in practice along dimensions of division of labor and responsibility, level of specialization and type of care technology, targeting of assistance, and temporal variation in practice norms as episodic or maintenance-oriented (Abrahams, Capitman, Leutz, & Macko, 1989). Related issues raised by this exploratory study include the patterns of differences in decisions of case managers within the same organization, differences from the organizational norm among individual case managers, and ways the particular care setting can influence which types of client need elicit greater or less response: medical *vs.* social *vs.* psychological needs; treatment *vs.* maintenance needs (Abrahams, Capitman, Leutz, & Macko, 1989).

Although it may be expected that the integrity of case management's integrative purpose is sustained across professional disciplines, the concept—or 'rubric'—of different case management models belies that expectation. For example, as suggested by the study described above and as observed in practice, the medical and legal case management models usually differ in at least one important respect from a social work case management model. Medical and legal case management services typically are delivered as extensions of the physician's or the attorney's office. Although other disciplines and resources are relied upon (Finkel & Rogers, 1992), these are viewed as ancillary to the provision of medical or legal services. The social work model of case management would seem to serve better the integrative purpose of this service. Ideally, in the social work model, no service is seen as subordinate to any other. Rather, each and every service is coordinated and delivered as reciprocally contributing to a shared goal of attaining the client's long-term well-being. Finkel and Rogers (1992) call for formal training in "the multi-disciplinary team approach" and for ongoing "psychiatric-care manager collaborations." Training is essential in order to promote better communication between specialists, and it should be implemented under a delivery systems perspective that avoids a hierarchical ordering of services.

The execution of agreements between provider agencies can help to mediate differences in organizations with respect to the targeting of services, specialization, and rules and regulations governing delivery of services. By specifying parameters and tasks for the client-based cooperation and collaboration between providers, inter-agency agreements serve to operationalize a coordinated approach to assisting clients in need of organizationally overlapping resources. The use of agreements treats coordination between agencies as a proactive, practicable service strategy, rather than as a well-meaning resolve that may not be translated into action.

THE CASE MANAGEMENT PROCESS

Case management is a process of needs assessment, coordinated planning and arrangement for service, and monitoring of the social care accessed according to a time-limited plan agreed to by the client and the case manager. Core case management tasks include:

Needs assessment: The case manager collects information about the client's social and physical environment, his/her ability to perform the personal and instrumental activities of daily life, and the availability and quality of informal caregiving resources that pertain to the client's functional status. Information about the client's situation is then evaluated by the case manager in partnership with the client and the client's family in order to specify client needs and problems for further formal and informal interventions.

Formulation of a service/care plan: The case manager and the client explore and agree upon service objectives and options available to the client in support of the agreed-upon service objectives.

Implementation of the service/care plan: The case manager may engage in the following activities for the arrangement and authorization of services: contact and coordination with providers, and ad hoc case conferences for the negotiation and coordination of service delivery to the client according to the agreed-upon service plan.

Follow-up and monitoring of service delivery: The case manager schedules and maintains telephone and face-to-face contacts with formal service providers, informal caregivers, and the client as necessary to ensure the timely initiation and maintenance of adequate care.

Reassessment of client needs: The case manager examines on a scheduled basis the client's use of services in order to respond to changes that may occur in the client's needs or in the availability and adequacy of the caregiving resources in place. Accordingly, the case manager and the client regularly update the services/care plan and may revise the pattern of services provided for in the plan. The case manager may reduce or terminate his or her active intervention upon the client's attainment of care plan goals.

Although the process necessarily includes the provision of information and usually of referrals to one or more service providers or entitlement bureaucracies, the major element that distinguishes the case management process from the information and referral interventions is the care plan, which should be based upon a thorough assessment of client needs and developed in partnership with the client or his or her representative.

Necessary to the efficient, effective implementation of the case management process are, of course, qualified personnel, clients or their representatives who are able and willing to participate in the process, and responsive provider systems. Herein lies a major case management challenge. Assuming the availability of adequately trained case managers who are personally and professionally committed to client-centered service and whose organization supports this commitment, the case management process may be jeopardized, truncated, misused, or abused because the client, the client's family, other concerned individuals, or provider systems cannot or will not participate appropriately. Information that is required for a sufficient assessment of need may not be supplied. Client agreement to release personal information to other helping agencies may not be given. There may be resistance to the exploration of service alternatives. Political influence may be exerted inappropriately. There may be conflicting values in relation to client self-determination or the equitable use of resources, or both. Response from entitlement bureaucracies or other sources of help may be lackadaisical, lackluster, or just lacking.

Case load pressures may introduce time constraints that may interfere with the case manager's maintenance of a calm, reasoned, systematic, thorough, and individuated approach to problem solving. The client's medical condition, physical and psychological functional status, or environmental situation may add up to life-threatening risk for the client, necessitating immediate decisions that will have a lasting and often an irreversible impact on whether the client can stay at home or must be institutionalized.

All these factors, as well as—perhaps most important— serious gaps in the availability of health and social care resources, may impinge on what should be a straightforward and orderly process of identifying and responding to need. Ideally, these factors are understood and addressed as part and parcel of a professionally guided problem solving process in which the complexities, ambiguities, and vagaries of human behavior are expected and accepted as contributing to creative and meaningful practice.

BUREAUCRATIZATION OF THE PROCESS

Public agencies, and probably most private agencies that operate with public monies, have numerous procedures in place to ensure the maintenance of complete and standardized records of service activities. Under the banner of accountability, service efforts are typically projected and measured in quantifiable units of activity and recipients served. Then, costs per unit of service and recipient are computed in terms of the total service effort projected and produced during a particular period of time. Certainly there is implicit pressure on practitioners to perform in accordance with quantified service levels. Often this pressure is explicit, as provider agencies compete for public and private funds on the basis of productivity measures that do not, per se, differentiate performance in terms of the quality of the effort produced. Further, in this accountability system, little attention may be given to monitoring and evaluating the impact of service effort on client needs; the differences in clients' lives resulting from service are not reflected in service statistics. The question of what good, if any, has been accomplished for X number of clients in X hours of activity is subordinated to a measurement of time on the job.

For a so-called "soft," that is, a personnel-intensive, type of case management, undue administrative emphasis on input and its quantification may generate a displaced sense of purpose which may lead to professional malaise. The considerable time involved in recording activity cuts into the time required to think and evaluate activity in terms of its impact on need. Case managers are at risk of viewing their responsibilities as primarily clerical ones. In such situations, the case manager's sense of professional accountability may be diluted or even destroyed.

In addition to paperwork and procedural requirements for recording their performance, case managers are also involved in helping clients with various entitlements like Medicaid, SSI, and Social Security. There is enormous paperwork in sorting out and applying the rules and regulations that affect eligibility for and benefits from these resources. The risk to the case management process in negotiating these highly specialized and bureaucratic programs is similar to that engendered by the previously described performance accountability paperwork.

In these negotiations, client need for a benefit may be subordinated or relegated to fiscally centered rather than need-centered considerations. For example, a person's ineligibility for a benefit that is based on his or her income and/ or assets profile may be viewed as a lack of need for that

benefit. Conversely, a client's financial eligibility for a benefit may result in an over-application of that benefit. Greater
need than exists may be assessed simply because financial
eligibility for the benefit has been established. The level of
public funding for a benefit may also affect an eligible
client's qualification for that benefit. In a scarce economy
the under-application of benefits is typical. Therefore, the
definition of need is budget-driven. Home care under medical assistance programs like Medicaid in New York State
and Medi-Cal in California is typical of public benefits affected by these fiscal factors. The case manager's challenge
is twofold in these situations. Attention to client need is in
danger of being subverted to macro- as well as micro-fiscal
considerations. In this context, the case manager's client-
centered focus is crucial. Only when the client's need has
been systematically, objectively, and individually established should feasibility or pragmatic factors, including fiscally driven eligibility and qualification, be addressed. This
is easier said than done!

THE COLLABORATIVE PROCESS

Fortunately, the case management process itself can be a
powerful countervailing force to mitigate the dogmatic approach to assistance which may result from bureaucratized
service delivery and accountability systems. The positive
force that the case management process can offer resides in
the opportunities for shared expertise and effort, often referred to as networking, or collegial coordination of performance within and among organizational systems. The effective coordination of services is a function of collegial
interaction between case managers within their own agencies and with representatives of other agencies and institutions that have a role in ameliorating client need. Collegial
interaction presupposes horizontal relationships of professionalism rather than hierarchical bureaucratic ones of positional authority, commonly known as chain of command.
Although a challenge, collegial decision making can be

achieved within or among entities whose formal organization is hierarchical. Client-centered attention on what has to be accomplished helps the case manager to keep the location of responsibility and authority in a proper perspective; focus should be on the means or obstacles to the achievement of client-centered service objectives, not on a predetermined limit of what can be accomplished.

Intra-Agency Collegiality

The following mechanisms for the promotion of collaborative decision making within an agency are recommended for the successful intra-organizational coordination of services. These mechanisms rely on the collegial sharing of expertise.

Quality Centers: Quality centers are established in various substantive service areas, such as housing, mental health, home care, caregiver resources, and protective services. Each area is assigned to a case manager for the development by that individual of special expertise therein. Through the sharing of their expertise in formal presentations to colleagues, ad hoc case conferences, and individual consults, case managers are able to rely on one another to supplement and strengthen in assigned areas the generic knowledge required of all case managers.

Case Intake and Assignment Meetings: Intake and case assignment meetings are participatory. Case managers take turns presenting to the group requests for service that have been received by the agency and lead deliberations as to initial strategies and the assignment of primary case responsibility. This team approach to organizing the response of the case management unit helps everyone to respond collectively and collegially to all others' individual interests, concerns, problems, professional strengths, helping styles, and constraints in relation to their work. Service principles and professional norms are reinforced by this mechanism, which is based on inter-dependence and consensus building.

Inter-Organizational Networking

A collegially based collaborative approach to service is a successful one for case management clients and representa-

tives of outside agencies and institutions, because in this
approach positional authority is not automatically equated
with superior knowledge and ability. Case managers are
socialized to feel comfortable about contacting and confer-
ring with anyone from the bottom to the top of an organizational hierarchy in order to obtain needed information,
advice, and resource determinations. In the spirit of shared
expertise and concern, confrontational and adversarial en-
counters are not viewed as effective strategies to meet client
need. Rather, areas of agreement are sought; there is a belief
in the ability to achieve consensus and a concomitant reliance on consensus building. The challenge to case managers
working within a collegial/networking model of professional
relationships is to overcome the resistance to networking
that may occur among colleagues, clients, and concerned
others who may appear to be intractably opposed to networking, and who, for whatever personal or other reason,
rely on position, political influence, or even the power of
obstinacy to achieve their aims. The opportunity in a networking model is for a more effective service outcome than
can be accomplished in a working model that relies solely
or primarily on positional authority or power. A collegial
networking model simply offers more possibilities for the
realization of service goals because, by definition, the network model is predicated on input from more sources than
is usual when positional determinations structure the case
management intervention. The sheer weight of collegial support can contravene even the most biased individual choice.

The Informal Caregivers

Although families and other informal or natural caregivers
are central to the ability of older people to manage at home,
these caregivers have not received significant substantive
support from government in their caregiving responsibilities. Some public funds have been allocated for the provision
of respite services and for the creation of caregiver resource
centers, but policy providing financial and other incentives

to encourage and sustain family caregiving is lacking. Therefore, much of the direct, formal assistance to natural caregivers is provided residually or peripherally by case managers whose primary client is considered to be the elderly person in need of convalescent or long-term community-based help. Informal caregivers also should receive the focused attention of case managers. Support of the concern and feelings of obligation exhibited by family caregivers should not be provided in either a residual or a peripheral fashion.

Although needs assessment instruments may include a section geared to identifying informal caregivers, these instruments are generally not helpful in focusing the case manager's attention on a differential assessment of the involvement of informal caregivers. Instead, willingness and ability to provide care should be ascertained, and the assumption that ability always accompanies willingness to provide care should be avoided. Ability should not only be assessed, but be promoted and facilitated by the case manager, who should provide information about formal caregiving resources, including respite care opportunities, peer support groups, and training in the techniques of caregiving. The case manager should supplement this information with guidance and assisted referrals so as to enable the informal caregiver to identify and access the formal services needed to support his or her caregiving. Personal assistance to the caregiver is especially important when the elderly care-recipient has cognitive disabilities, including those that are due to Alzheimer's disease or are developmentally based. The case manager should also assess caregiver burden, whatever the extent of the caregiver's current or anticipated responsibility. The same responsibilities might be stressful to one caregiver, but not to another. Further, willingness and ability to sustain care may differ for spouses, adult daughters, adult sons, nieces, nephews, and siblings.

The central practice issues for case managers are, first, to develop an awareness that informal caregiving is an important factor in the ability of many elderly to avoid institutionalization for long-term care, and, then, to treat informal caregivers as individually as the elderly client. The challenge to case management services is to develop strategies for the differential assessment and support of informal caregiving. One such strategy might be to seek referrals from hospitals of patients being discharged to the care of a spouse or other relative. Prior to discharge, the relative's willingness and ability to provide care could be assessed and enabled. Then, if necessary, caregiving alternatives and/or supplemental resources could be developed in order to avoid undue stress and burden to both the patient and his or her informal caregivers. Even in situations where informal caregiving has preceded hospitalization, change at discharge in a patient's functional needs requires a thorough reassessment of the caregiving situation.

CONCLUSION

This chapter has touched upon the major aspects of case management which shape its practice as dynamic and challenging, with the opportunity for case managers to develop the knowledge and skills necessary to operate on many levels simultaneously. Case management professionals have a central role in promoting, strengthening, and sustaining the ability of older people to remain in their homes and communities and to avoid the crippling emotional and financial costs of institutional dependency.

NOTES

1. The reader is referred to a supplementary issue of *Generations*, the journal of the American Society on Aging, that is devoted entirely to the long–term-care practitioner's role in regard to patient/client autonomy (Hofland, 1990).

2. The reader is referred to Helen Harris Perlman's moving exposition of the usefulness and dynamics of such a helping relationship in her book *Relationship, the Heart of Helping People* (1979).

REFERENCES

Abrahams, R., Capitman, J., Leutz, W., & Macko, P. (1989). Variations in care planning practice in the social/HMO: An exploratory study. *The Gerontologist, 29*(6), 725–736.

Finkel, S., & Rogers, S. (1992). A clinical collaboration of a psychiatrist and a geriatric care manager. *Journal of Case Management, 1*(2), 49–52.

Generations. (1990). Autonomy and long term care practice. *14*(Suppl.), 1–96.

Morris, R. (1989). Challenges of aging in tomorrow's world: Will gerontology grow, stagnate, or change? *The Gerontologist, 29*(4), 494–500.

Perlman, H. H. (1979). *Relationship, the heart of helping people.* Chicago: The University of Chicago Press.

9

Impact of the Environment on Agencies Serving Older Adults

Roslyn H. Chernesky

TODAY MILLIONS OF OLDER AMERICANS are receiving care and services from a vast network of human service agencies, their workers, and volunteers. In too many instances, however, service is provided despite being encumbered on a daily basis. Agencies and workers confront constraints on their practice, barriers to effective service delivery, and obstacles that determine who can receive service, for what duration, and in what form. Sadly, the struggle to provide services under conditions that hinder or even preclude quality care is likely to be the state of affairs for some time to come. Human services face an overall decline in support and a general increase in assaults which are nurtured by a conservative climate.

More than ever, it is clear that the situation of human service organizations, including agencies that serve older adults, is determined by the environment in which they operate. Some agencies are concerned with surviving; others are searching for ways to offer the same or more services with considerably fewer resources. Managers of these agencies must reconsider what they can actually do, and do effectively, under the circumstances. It will continue to be a difficult and painful time, but also a challenging one, for both agency managers and workers as they struggle to respond and adapt to the demands and pressures they confront. How well they do so will be a critical factor in the effective provision of services and programs necessary to meets the needs of older adults.

In this chapter I will describe the external environment of

agencies serving older adults, the environment that determines what services are delivered and to whom. First, I will examine the aging service delivery network itself so that we may appreciate the influence wielded by multiple interest groups who have a stake in whether and how the elderly receive services. Second, I will review some of recent developments in this environment—the shifts in interests, competing values, changes in policies, the increase in client demand, and the decrease in financial and personnel resources.

To enhance the capacity of agencies serving older adults in these times, managers and workers must understand their agencies' environment, that is, the demands and pressures on managers and workers that shape their practice and services as well as the challenges and opportunities that are offered for effective service delivery. Such an understanding will be useful to workers who too readily tend to blame the client, themselves, or their immediate superiors for perceived failures and difficulties in responding to client needs. They will be able to see that factors outside their agencies constrain their professional activities and effectiveness. Managers too will recognize the political arena of service organizations with its determinants of organizational survival and quality service provision. Managers will be better able to avoid the inherent nature of the double-bind situation, thereby satisfying external pressures while simultaneously providing high-quality services.

The Agency's External Environment

The Aging Network

All agencies are part of a service delivery network through which they are interrelated to other agencies and organizations, usually in a given geographic area. It is through the network that services are made available to specific populations, such as older adults. The network includes all organizations that are essential for an agency to carry out its work.

It consists of other organizations that can refer clients to an agency and can accept clients from an agency. It also consists of individuals, groups, and organizations that control resources needed to provide services, such as personnel, funds for staff, materials, and supplies. The theory and practice of inter-organizational relations, which I can only briefly address here, constitute a large body of literature, attesting to the complexity and the importance of an organization's link to its environment and to the effective delivery of services (Aldrich, 1979; Levine & White, 1961; Pfeffer & Salancik, 1978).

The service delivery network for older adults includes the vast array of agencies that provide direct services to the elderly such as senior centers, long–term-care facilities, adult day-care centers, home-care agencies, and hospitals. The aging network, referred to more than a decade ago as "the aging enterprise" (Estes, 1979), comprises governmental or public organizations, such as state and county offices for aging, which are chartered by law and supported by public funds (taxes); not-for-profit voluntary or private agencies, such as family-service agencies, settlement houses, and many medical centers; and for-profit proprietary agencies, most often found among residential facilities and home-care agencies, whose aim is to make profits for their owners while providing services to the elderly. The network includes agencies whose sole mission is to provide services to older adults as well as to organizations that serve the elderly along with other populations or in addition to other activities.

Each agency in the network establishes its domain, which defines the areas in which the organization will function, what services it can and will offer, to whom, and how. This definition is both the agency's public promise about services it will provide and its claim to governmental and private resources. Some domains are clear, such as that of Senior Action in a Gay Environment (SAGE), a multi-service agency which serves only older gay and lesbian individuals. A skilled nursing facility is understood to differ from an adult home in terms of who can or cannot be accepted, and what services clients can expect to receive. In these instances, network agencies know to whom they can make referrals or from whom they can expect referrals. Other agency domains are less clear, and even ambiguous. Broad domains are confusing, but because these agencies claim they can offer a wide range of services, they can attract more clients and can take advantage of more funding sources. The boundaries separating agencies are generally understood; however, even though network agencies are expected to confine their practice to their domains, this is often not the case.

Agencies in the network usually know where gaps in services exist, what needs are unmet, which services are duplicated or unnecessary, and which agencies are not doing what they claim. Agencies informally monitor one another, and make judgments that can result in a refusal to collaborate or even in a withholding of clients. In general, agencies cooperate with one another because it is in their best interests to do so. A few agencies may collaborate formally, perhaps through referral agreements, joint sponsorship of programs, or working together as part of a coalition or task force to assess the needs of a segment of the elderly population such as the home-based elderly. Because agencies also compete which one another for clients, funding, or staff, inter-agency collaboration and coordination are difficult to achieve (Neugeboren, 1990).

Not all agencies in a service delivery network are equal. Some agencies are more dependent on the network, whereas others, usually because they control a valuable resource, such as operating funds, have greater influence and power. Because of their privileged position, these agencies can set rules the others must play by. Local offices of aging, for example, although service providers, can also disburse monies through contracted or purchased services. Therefore, they have far greater influence in an aging network than many other providers. Hospitals that discharge older patients to nursing homes wield power as long as nursing homes with empty beds are competing for their patients. In a supplier's market, this relationship will be just the opposite. If there are no beds in nursing homes yet hospitals must discharge patients to avoid being penalized for keeping patients beyond the time considered medically necessary, nursing homes can be selective; hospitals are then dependent upon the actions of the nursing homes.

Multiple Constituencies

The aging network comprises not only the agencies that actually deliver services, but also all the agencies and organizations that make it possible for agencies to deliver services. These organizations or constituent groups are mainly involved in issues related to the acquisition and allocation of resources and to accountability. They include funding agencies, regulatory bodies, and policy-making organizations, each of which has a stake in, places demands on, and expects results from the agencies. Consequently, these organizations wield extensive power over whether and how services are given and to whom.

Figure 1 depicts the multiple constituents of typical human service agencies. The ten constituent groups that make up an agency's environment surround the internal core of the agency, as shown in the center of the figure, and impact on the agency's administrators, human service workers, and support staff (Martin & O'Connor, 1989). Clients can be viewed as either an external constituent group or as part of or member of the organization. In this figure, the location of "individual clients" places clients as one of the ten multiple constituents. Where clients are placed would depend upon how clients relate to a particular agency, and how an agency relates to its clients. Older adults who are clients or consumers are more likely to be considered part of the environment if, by placing demands on agencies, they influence how services are delivered. Each of the multiple constituents is linked to the agency and has a stake in what it does. Each has the potential to support, hinder, or prevent agencies from providing services. Agencies are ultimately dependent upon these groups for survival.

By observing the way in which a service delivery network operates, one can see that many agency decisions are influenced by the interests of particular network members or of

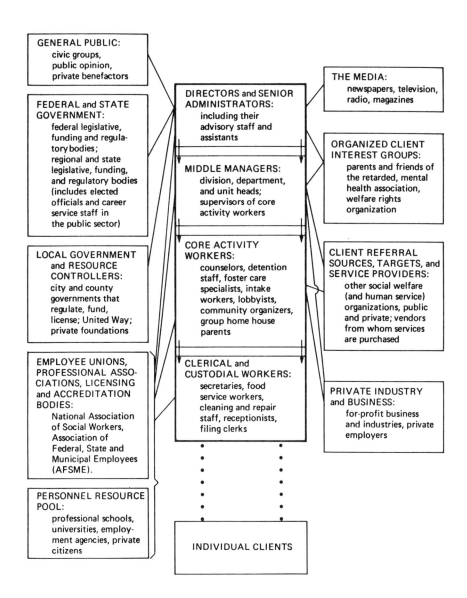

FIGURE 1. The Multiple Constituents of Social Welfare Organizations.
Note. From *The Social Environment: Open Systems Applications* (p. 204) by Patricia Yancey Martin and Gerald G. O'Connor. Copyright © 1989 by Longman Publishing Group. Reprinted with permission from Longman Publishing Group.

the network itself. The availability of new funding may lead agencies into new and different programming areas. A drop in funding can affect the size of workers' case loads. A change in reimbursement pattern may determine which clients are seen or given priority. A lack of trained and qualified personnel may result in the hiring of non-professionals concomitant with a change in job descriptions, a perfunctory handling of cases, a greater need for supervision, and eventually a different composition of clients served. Program expansion to field offices or outposting of existing service programs to new communities or sites is usually associated with increased allocations that are likely to be stable and secure from sources such as United Way. In fact, organizational change itself is most often associated with receiving new or additional revenue (Wernet & Austin, 1991).

If workers look at any aspect of how agency services are provided, it is likely they can trace the derivation of the policy or practice to a constituent interest within the agency's network. Doing so will help demonstrate how dependent agencies are on their environments. Human service organizations are placed in the untenable position of always having to react to events in their environments and to adapt to the demands of network resources providers. Successful adaptation permits organizational survival and determines the effectiveness of the services provided. Unfortunately, the more responsive agencies are to the wishes and needs of those constituents who control resources, the less responsive they may be to both staff and client interests (Martin, 1980).

CHARACTERISTICS OF THE EXTERNAL ENVIRONMENT

Although the relationships and the dynamics between network members and constituents' interests help explain much of how services are delivered, workers' constraints on practice, and obstacles to effective service delivery, in reality, the environment of agencies serving the elderly is far more complex. The environment is neither stable nor consistent; rather, it is in a state of flux, continuously shifting and changing. New pressures may arise, confronting agencies with differing and perhaps competing demands: some clear, others ambiguous; some friendly, others hostile. Through understanding the larger context of the environment, it is possible to appreciate fully what managers and workers must contend with on an almost daily basis.

A Changing Environment

An agency's environment is always changing. Its turbulence is brought about by emerging social, economic, and technological trends; shifts in funding priorities and programming interests; and changes in ideological or value preferences. Most often the changing environment is reflected in new or different public policies. In recent years, many mandated public policies were derived from fiscal policies related to cost containment.

One of the most dramatic public policy shifts impacting on the aging service delivery network relates to long-term care. The initiative taken by many states to change from a long-term residential care model to a community-based long–term-care system led to development of new agencies, new funding patterns, and new intervention models. This shift led to the growth of the home-care industry. The number of home-care providers is estimated today at 12,000 to 14,000 with for-profit agencies now accounting for about one-third of the total. Projections of total spending for services and products suggest that home care is now a $16 billion a year industry (Applebaum & Phillips, 1990).

The rapid expansion of adult day-care centers in the past decade can also be attributed to the same shift in public policy, as the federal government decided to encourage and make funds available for alternatives to institutional care. Not only did it lead to new and different provider agencies in the aging field, but the volume of clients for these centers increased. Moreover, many clients were in a more disabled condition when they came for care than were past day-care clients, and they needed more intensive care for longer periods of time (Wood, 1989).

New legislation changed the environment as well. The 1987 amendments to the Older Americans Act of 1965 required the addition of services for the prevention of abuse of older individuals as a priority for government funding. State offices on aging were required to indicate the agencies involved in identifying, preventing, and treating abused, neglected, and exploited elders and to determine the extent of unmet service needs. The subsequent creation of community-based Elder Abuse Task Forces had, in many instances, "a radiating impact on state law, the statewide adult protection service system, and regional policymaking bodies" (Foelker, Holland, Marsh, & Simmons, 1990).

Alternative reimbursement systems also changed the environment. Changes in Medicare financing incentives such as the Prospective Payment System (PPS), under which hospitals are reimbursed according to a predetermined amount for a predetermined length of stay for each medical diagnosis, affected hospital inpatient care and discharge planning across the country. They also led to greater competition in the growing market in care for older adults beyond conventional approaches to care. Hospitals, for example, developed a variety of case management services for impaired elderly people, many of which were initially supported by the Robert Wood Johnson Foundation's Program for Hospital Initiatives in Long-Term Care (MacAdam, et al., 1989).

New York State's Medicaid rules, known as RUGS (Resource Utilization Groups), determine reimbursement for nursing home patients and represent another example of the impact of reimbursement systems. When the flat rate for reimbursing Medicaid patients in nursing homes was discontinued in 1986, the new system, which pays homes a fixed rate based upon the average level of functioning of all the patients in the home, led nursing homes to favor admission of less functional patients with healthcare needs in order to get higher rate of Medicaid reimbursement (Abend-Wein, 1991).

Another general shift occurred in emphasis from developing and expanding service delivery networks to ensuring that networks actually work. New structures emerged to maintain and to make better use of the networks rather than to provide additional or improved direct services. They included informal inter-organizational committees as well as formally structured inter-organizational councils and planning bodies, all of which were intended to overcome the lack of coordination typical of service networks. Other examples of efforts to improve the service delivery network included the use of uniform admissions assessments, linkage agreements, common program-data systems, and ombudsman systems that serve as complaint and advocacy resources for those having problems with the network's operation (Austin, 1991).

Efforts encouraging agencies to deliver services through collaboration and not through single agency auspices were also aimed at improving service networks. The early and basic principle of the Administration on Aging (AOA) to establish partnerships between the public and private sectors (Tolliver, 1988) is now an almost universal expectation among other governmental funders as well. Interest in collaboration is also emphasized by foundation grantmakers. For example, the 1986 Request for Proposals (RFP) for the Living-at-Home projects, a major multi–foundation-supported endeavor, specifically asked for lead agencies such as visiting nurse associations, hospitals, and area agencies on aging to establish a partnership with other community organizations, either non-profit or proprietary. The purpose of the Living-at-Home projects was to develop cooperative networks of multiple health and social services providers in order to increase access to care, to reduce duplication of services, and to identify and fill service gaps (Hughes & Guihan, 1989).

Case management, a model of service delivery that gained popularity in the 1980s, is perhaps the best example of this shift in interest from expanding networks to ensuring that they are effective. Monk claims that "case management is the inevitable corollary of an age of service specialization and of a service system which does not facilitate easy access" (1990, p. 13). Case management primarily involves gaining access to and negotiating services from a variety of formal and informal sources on behalf of individuals in need of services. As with information and referral agencies in the 1970s which were designed to increase access to services, case management is based on the assumption that necessary services exist in the network and that individuals require only to be linked to appropriate services for their needs to be met.

Emphasis on the "privatization" of human services, buttressed by President Bush's strong position that business and industry could play a significant role in service delivery, represents another change in the environment. Whereas collaboration with the profit sector was encouraged in the past, the shift now is to have the profit sector take over services heretofore provided by either the voluntary or the public sector under the assumption that the private sector can do the job as well, if not better, and at less cost. We see this thrust in the aging field with the emergence of life-care or continuing-care retirement communities as attractive alternatives to nursing homes for the provision of long-term care. By the mid-1980s, 275 life-care communities housed 100,000 elders as part of the commercial eldercare movement that has been expanding despite cutbacks in federal funding (Stoesz, 1989). Hospitals too are linking the elderly's need for personal care services with retirement housing that they own, lease, or manage, having found partners among nursing home operators, real estate developers, and hotel companies.

Even grantmakers, who actually contribute a very small proportion of income to human service agency budgets, impact on the environment when they change funding priorities or their grantmaker roles as they did in the 1980s (Schreter & Brummel, 1989). Reflecting the increasing concern about the rising costs of health care and the need for long-term care, foundation funding to the aging field in 1985 went primarily to health care, with a heavy emphasis on cost containment (Mahoney, 1989). Just recently, two of the nation's largest private foundations in the health and aging fields, the Robert Wood Johnson Foundation and the Henry J. Kaiser Family Foundation, announced a switch in emphasis to grants aimed at making federal and state health programs more responsive to people's needs. This shift represents a significant departure from the traditional reluctance of foundations to work directly with government (Bailey, 1989). Heightened grantmaker interest in intergenerational programs during the 1980s which resulted in many agencies proposing the creation of such programs further illustrates the influence of foundations.

A Hostile Environment

The human services environment can be friendly and supportive, but in general it is hostile. More favorable environments are found in those situations where an agency's services cost the taxpayer nothing and are considered desirable or consistent with society's values. Several agencies serving the elderly operate in a friendlier environment, facing few threats. For these agencies, survival of the agency is not a major issue. That is not to say that agencies in friendly environments need not be wary or prepare for changes in sentiment about their worthiness. But managers can devote greater attention to internal agency operations and less time to trying to placate, buffer, and adapt to assaults from the environment. And workers can more easily carry out their work and feel better about it.

Agencies serving the elderly are increasingly faced with a hostile environment, especially as ageism grows. Streib and Binstock (1990) suggest that in the late 1970s as possible burdensome economic and social implications of an aging population became apparent, compassionate popular stereotypes of the aging as disadvantaged began to erode. Older persons began to be viewed as prosperous, hedonistic, and selfish. This new stereotype of older people coincided with escalating costs of health care, which were attributed to the elderly, and it was not difficult to conclude that older persons were no longer in need (or deserving) of publicly or privately supported programs.

Local funding for human services is often given begrudgingly. Frequently, local dollars must be given because of mandated matching federal or state funding requirements as with Medicaid. Tax dollars collected from wage earners are being dispensed, it is viewed, to individuals who either should have had the foresight to save for the future or should be taken care of by their own families instead of by the public. Even programs that help older adults become employed are suspect. Despite evidence to the contrary, the elderly are seen as jeopardizing jobs that could be taken by younger, able workers. On the other hand, efforts to use the experience and skills of older adults in volunteer endeavors are highly regarded and therefore operate in a more supportive environment.

Even services to older adults that are generally seen as acceptable may face hostility. Because of the recent emphasis on elder abuse, adult-protective services are involved in investigating and exposing a problem that society generally does not want to know about or believe happens in their community. Support for these services is given reluctantly although it is publicly endorsed. Society's expectation that human services be accountable and efficient, although not necessarily wrong, reflects a hostile environment. Since the 1970s, human service agencies have operated in a environment where they must continually demonstrate that their expenditures are neither wasteful nor inefficient. Quality assurance programs to examine systematically and continuously the quality of services, identify deficiencies, and take corrective action are mandated by many accrediting bodies and are now required for participation in many state and federal programs. This emphasis confirms that purchasers of services have the right as well as the responsibility to examine the services and to judge them for compliance, standards, and quality. It also confirms that funders of human services have a right to say how, when, where, and to whom services will be delivered. Thus, the interests of the funders—whether the public-at-large who support agency services through tax dollars; owners and managers of for-profit organizations; or United Way contributors, individual donors, or foundations that support voluntary agencies— take precedence over what may actually be best for clients.

One example of how client needs may have been disregarded because of the emphasis placed on accountability and efficiency is the impact of the Diagnostic Related Groupings (DRGs) on older adults discharged from hospitals. Introduced to curtail the rapidly escalating costs of hospitalization, the Medicaid reimbursement procedures were designed to pay hospitals only for the length of patient-stay predetermined appropriate for each medical diagnosis and were supposed to maintain an adequate level of quality care. Many were concerned that as a result of the reimbursement formula older patients would be discharged sooner and in far greater need of care, especially since hospitals would be financially penalized if they could not medically justify keeping patients for any extra length of time.

COMPETING VALUES AND DEMANDS

Cost Containment

The environment of agencies can also be characterized as one of competing values and demands, pulling agencies in and from many directions (Edwards & Austin, 1991). There are two major competing values and demands in the environment of agencies serving the elderly today. One is the conflict between cost containment and quality care which is represented in a number of national policies and in regulations especially in reaction to reimbursement of services. Some of these were noted earlier—RUGS, PPS, DRGs. The same conflict can be seen today in the growth of managed care.

Community-based long-term care as an alternative to institutional care was essentially a cost containment policy. Throughout the mid-1980s, a number of demonstration programs were sponsored by the Health Care Financing Administration (HCFA) to make the most appropriate yet cost-effective long–term-care services available to the elderly by "channeling" them using case management (Capitman, Haskins, & Bernstein, 1986). Although community-based long-term care was pronounced a priority domestic policy, the federal government's desire to reduce the ever-increasing Medicare and Medicaid costs contributed to the failure to develop a true community long-term continuum for the aged and to an increased burden of long-term care on individuals and families (Kirwin, 1988). At the same time, efforts to make community-based care cost-effective through targeting, triage, or less intensive case management were encouraged, despite growing evidence from studies and demonstration programs that substituting community-based services for institutional care costs more than is saved (Eggert, Friedman, & Zimmer, 1990; Kemper, 1990).

Today, agencies operate in a climate of increased pressure to demonstrate that they are cost-effective, neither wasteful nor inefficient, and that they are taking advantage of all possible funding avenues, including client fees for service. The pressure can easily have deleterious effects: maintaining a low-cost and less skilled labor pool, selecting clients who have financial resources over those who do not, and replacing necessary but high-cost services with less costly and less satisfactory arrangements.

Increase in Clients and Demand for Services

The second major competing value and demand in the environment of agencies serving older adults is the expectation that with fewer and fewer resources the aging network will and can provide services to increasing numbers of clients.

Demographic shifts in the past decade alone would account for the rapid increase in the number of elderly persons requiring and seeking services. But other factors also contributed to the rise in real and potential clients making demands upon the aging service network. Older adults were seen as a less homogeneous group. As their diversity was recognized, policymakers, funders, and agencies separated the elderly and their problems into heterogeneous categories. Differences between the groups of the aged, such as the young-old and the old-old, supported different programming needs. The earlier service's focus on people between 65 and

75 shifted as the significant increase in the numbers of very aged men and women attracted unprecedented attention during the past decade (Achenbaum, 1991). A recent study of the needs of the elderly in the 21st century suggests there will be a dramatic increase in the number of frail elderly persons aged 85 years or more, a growth in the prevalence of disability among the elderly, a sizable group of older adults at serious financial risk, and a dramatic increase in the need for supportive services (Zedlewski, 1989).

Providers such as senior centers which traditionally did not target services to specific groups but served almost any older adult interested in their activities were called upon to do more for target groups, especially the frail, low-income, and disabled elderly minorities (Cox & Monk, 1990; Krout, Cutler, & Coward, 1990).

The "discovery" of Alzheimer's disease led to a new client group which made heavy demands on services to older adults. It precipitated the development of new organizations, providers, and services which became part of and made demands upon the aging network. The Alzheimer's Association alone has 207 chapters in 49 states with a national budget of $17.5 million, engages 35,000 volunteers, and sponsors over 1,500 support groups through its local chapters. There are 15 Alzheimer's disease research centers supported by federal research funding, and 39 states have Alzheimer's disease–specific programs funded at over $23 million (Lombardo & McConnell, 1990).

Other problems common to the general population created additional client groups and service demands when they involved older adults. For example, pressures on the aging network to integrate elderly persons with mental retardation into their services occurred with the increased longevity of persons with mental retardation. The trend toward the expansion of age-specialized programs for older persons with mental retardation was further formalized by the provisions in the 1987 amendments to both the Older Americans Act and the Developmental Disabilities Act intended to facilitate collaboration between both service networks (Seltzer, Krauss, Litchfield, & Modlish, 1989). The

aging network is also being asked to better address the needs
of the blind and visually impaired elderly (Biegel, Petchers,
Snyder, & Beisgen, 1989). Considering that 1 out of 10 AIDS
patients is at least 50 years old, approximately 1% to 10% of
the older population are alcoholics, and the numbers of
homeless elderly are rapidly increasing, we can anticipate
more and more clients who will expect their needs to be met
by agencies serving the elderly.

Because of the aging network's concern with those affected by the aging of others, it has assumed responsibility
for providing services to support and relieve family caregivers. Respite care to help those who care for elderly people
with dementia developed over the past decade. This commitment to caregivers is expected to grow since the demographics suggests that it will become increasingly common for
younger elder persons to provide some kind of support for
"old-old" parents and they will have few siblings with whom
to share such responsibilities. Yet to be explored is the place
of the aging network on behalf of the fast-growing numbers
of older adults who are raising families once again by assuming full child-caring responsibilities for their grandchildren.

New problems, new technologies, and new policy mandates bring new clients and new demands for services to
which the service delivery network tries to respond. An
excellent example is the increased demand for home care.
After the implementation of Medicare's Diagnostic Related
Group (DRG) provisions, area agencies on aging indicated a
196% increase in skilled health care in the home and a 69%
increase in housekeeping or homemaking. Both length of
services and number of services per client increased for most
agencies where DRGs were in effect (Monk, 1990).

INCREASE IN NETWORK SIZE, DIVERSITY, AND COMPLEXITY

An overall increase in the numbers of older adults who
required care as well as greater demands upon existing
agencies and programs inevitably led to an expansion of the
aging service network. Over the years we have seen a prolif-

eration of agencies, programs, and services on behalf of older adults. As Morris (1989) notes, these organizations, agencies, and professions make up a large infrastructure of thousands of national and local agencies that employ over two million professional and support workers and a large superstructure for the field of gerontology. Several factors account for this growth.

The 1965 Older Americans Act (OAA) spearheaded the rapid growth of a service delivery network comprising services ranging from social change and advocacy through restorative, developmental, and preventive services via the Administration on Aging's (AOA) network of state and area agencies on aging and the mobilization of others to provide these services (Tolliver, 1988).

More than 125 departments in the federal government and numerous agencies at the state level have programs designed to serve the elderly. Some examples are the Urban Mass Transportation Authority, the U.S. Department of Housing and Urban Development, the U.S. Department of Energy, and the Health Care Financing Agency (Tolliver, 1988). Yet there are gaps in services because of eligibility criteria, difficulty in access, lack of knowledge about what is available, or the failure to use services considered "welfare." A wide range of services were developed in response to these gaps. These include information and referral agencies, mobile delivery of health services, alternative health programs, and on-site services such as senior centers and entitlement counseling at senior housing projects. An excellent example of a recent growth spurred by gaps in services is the establishment of private case management agencies that serve at the request of family members who are unable to meet the needs of their elderly relations on a daily basis.

The service network has also grown in response to the demands of national, regional, and local citizen advocates for less traditional and more innovative services. For example, some have called for more social change, less bureaucracy, nonprofessional rather than professional staff, and mutual-help groups. In response, the 1980s saw a rapid increase in alternative agencies, organized to meet in more

flexible ways a broad array of needs not met by older established agencies (Perlmutter, 1988). Hospices, for example,
represent alternative organizations in the field of aging, as
their primary aim is to promote a unique approach to
serving the dying and their families (Gummer, 1988).

Organizations that previously did not serve the elderly
have entered the field in recent years. Some responded to
the changing demographics they experienced in their case
loads; others responded to new funding opportunities. Uni-
versities, for example, now offer gerontology higher education programs and geriatric specializations in medical
schools, sponsor social research centers or institutes, and
conduct special degree or continuing education programs
targeted to seniors. Hospitals and medical centers have established specialized geriatric inpatient units oriented
toward assessment and rehabilitation.

In addition, AOA's emphasis in the 1980s on models of
public/private sponsorship has brought corporations into
the aging field not just as funders but also as active participants in the delivery of services. Corporations are establishing eldercare programs to address problems arising from
the increasing involvement of workers in caring for older
family members which impact on productivity, the quality
of work, and morale. Some insurance companies are beginning to provide case management to policy holders who
experience difficulty with daily living activities. IBM alone
is expected to eventually invest up to $3 million as part of
the IBM Elder Care Project Development Fund in communities where its employees live and work (IBM Funds, 1991).

The network composition has also been affected by an
increase in nongovernmental funders of aging programs.
During the 1980s the number of foundations giving in the
field of aging increased from 209 in 1983 to 263 in 1987—
this reflects a 26% increase. Overall, taking into consideration those foundations which gave only one grant during
that period as well as those which gave more consistently, a
total of 415 different foundations supported aging programs
(Greenberg, Gutheil, Parker, & Chernesky, 1991). Although
these foundations gave relatively little money compared to

both annual federal funding in aging and total foundation giving in all areas, these grantmakers represented new, and potentially powerful, participants in the environment of agencies serving older adults.

The increase in network size, diversity, and complexity has created a number of problems that adversely affect the delivery of services to the elderly. Specialization and fragmentation resulting from the proliferation of agencies and organizations is confusing to both provider agencies and clients. Each organization brings its own eligibility rules and its own belief as to what is best for clients, making it difficult to understand and negotiate the maze of rules. Each is administered separately, with its own forms and paperwork, although each seeks the same basic information. In order to make the cumbersome system work better, additional layers of organization have been introduced—information, referral, ombudsman, advocacy, case management—to assist with access and utilization. As Morris states, "the sheer complexity of the provider system may, paradoxically, increase the volume of unmet need as much as it increases the variety of services" (1989, p. 497), as more cracks develop between specialties. As a result, many, including frail aged members in community settings, face formidable problems acquiring needed services and are often isolated, neglected, and out of touch with the network of services organized to respond to their needs (Kirwin, 1988).

REDUCTION IN FINANCIAL RESOURCES

Annual federal funding in aging in the mid 1980s was just over $250 billion for Social Security, Medicare and Medicaid, Supplemental Security Income (SSI), retirement benefits and pensions, programs run by the Administration on Aging, and research conducted by the National Institute on Aging. This support was suddenly placed in jeopardy with the 1981 Omnibus Reconciliation Act and the conservative climate of the decade. The keystone of President Reagan's 1980 campaign was that public spending was out of control.

Reagan promised to limit Washington's concerns to areas where the federal government had only a constitutional responsibility, thus conveying an anti-liberal and anti-government position (Achenbaum, 1991). Many conservative policies that would have affected older adults and their entitlements were thwarted by powerful coalitions representing them, including "Save Our Security" (SOS), the AFL-CIO, and the National Organization for Women. Nevertheless, changes in how federal monies were distributed at the state and local levels and in restrictions affecting criteria and reimbursement had the overall effect of reducing public federal spending for social programs, including services for older adults.

The general decline in the nation's economy and the conservative climate, both of which have contributed to the public's unwillingness to pay more taxes, are unlikely to change in the near future. We now recognize that the declining economic condition in the U.S. is not a temporary phenomenon. As Edwards and Yankey (1991a) suggest, the human services have entered a new era of fiscal austerity, and it is a dramatic change after nearly 50 years of uninterrupted growth. The financial consequences of Ronald Reagan's "New Federalism," the Gramm-Rudman-Hollings legislation with its mandated balanced federal budget, and the 1990 OBRA which established new deficit-reduction targets until 1995 will be felt by agencies throughout the 1990s.

Because federal resources are likely to remain scarce for the remainder of this century, how funds are allocated will be important to the aging network. It has been noted that during the 1976–1986 period, the federal government already altered its fiscal commitment to education and research programs in the field of aging. Federal support for research and training in the social and behavioral aspects of aging dropped whereas funding for aging biomedical education and research fared relatively well, representing a dramatic shift in federal emphasis (Kerin, Estes, & Douglass, 1989).

State and local governments are struggling under the burden of staggering social problems as well as deep federal cuts. Like the federal government, their deficits are rapidly increasing. The general decline in the nation's economy contributes to a public unwillingness to pay more taxes for the funding of human services. Services are being slashed, and are not being favored even where there has been caring and liberal executive leadership. Unable to raise additional funds with a tax increase, states have no alternative but to reduce budgets. State and local governments can no longer be depended upon to buffer the impact of federal cuts by substituting local tax revenue as many had been able to do in the early 1980s, Instead, agencies are now trying to decrease the impact of state and local cuts by continuing to provide programs when public contracts are dropped from their own tight budgets.

The fear that the loss of federal support was imminent in the early 1980s led agencies serving older adults to increase their efforts to obtain greater foundation support. This strategy was successful. The aging field obtained a greater proportion of total foundation giving from 1983 to 1987 than previously (Greenberg, Gutheil, Parker, & Chernesky, 1991). But foundations were already unable to respond to a growing number of social problems and did not view their role as keeping programs alive by making up the money lost through federal, state, or local government funding cuts.

Foundation giving for the field of aging in the 1990s may not be any better, but it may not be any worse. A recent study of grantmakers suggests that the field will continue to hold its own in the face of the many compelling needs that grantmakers must address when allocating funds (Gutheil & Chernesky, 1991). Yet, trends and developments in foundation giving suggest that less money will be available for general operating and continuing support, although foundations will continue to give grants for the development of new programs (Bailey, 1989). Foundations are giving larger grants and are giving for multiple-year rather than one-year projects. Increasingly, foundations are setting funding priorities and targeting their grants accordingly. Together, these practices will result in fewer agencies' and fewer programs' receiving foundation support each year.

A WORK FORCE IN SHORT SUPPLY

Funding is not the only declining resource in the environment of agencies serving the elderly, although perhaps it is its most valuable one. Another critical resource for labor-intensive human services is its work force, which is increasingly in short supply. It is unlikely that there will be enough qualified candidates to fill all the jobs in human services in the 1990s. Several factors contribute to the situation.

First, there is an increasingly tight labor market because fewer people are available to actually enter the work force. Second, those who do enter, especially low-level workers, are expected to have deficiencies in basic skills. Third, the continuing expansion of services in both the proprietary and the public sectors has increased the demand for human service personnel and the competition for a quality work force (Ewalt, 1991). Finally, efforts to recruit and retain staff are in competition with other fields such as sales and fast-food restaurants, both of which can offer similar (perhaps even better) salaries, benefits, and working conditions to agencies serving the elderly. In fact, the nationwide shortage of home health aides can be attributed to low wages, few fringe benefits, erratic hours, and the absence of a career track.

The estimate of the National Institute on Aging that 50,000 social workers will be serving the elderly by the year 2000 may be conservative. Where these social workers will come from, and how they will be prepared or retrained remain critical questions for the social work profession (Peterson, 1990). According to recent reports published by the Association for Gerontology in Higher Education, too few social workers are trained to meet the special needs of the elderly, and many social workers, like most other professionals, have been reluctant to serve the elderly ("Too Few Trained," 1991).

Volunteers are likely to be in short supply as well in the coming years. Agencies that rely upon an unpaid work force to deliver their services may have as much trouble recruiting and retaining volunteers as those that employ workers. As economic conditions require more individuals to enter the work force, especially women, it is likely that fewer people will be available to volunteer. Those who do volunteer are likely to be more selective about where they volunteer and what kind of volunteer work they choose.

IMPLICATIONS FOR AGENCIES

The picture presented here is grim. We can take with us an image of agencies battered and bruised especially if they are minor actors in an environment where others wield the power and control the resources that are necessary for effective service provision. But the image of passive and reactive agencies, adapting to their environments in order to prosper or even to survive, is a distorted one. It overlooks the agency as a significant player that shapes and manages the environment, and creatively takes advantage of the unintended opportunities therein.

The realization that human service agencies are dependent on their environments, but that the extent and nature of this dependency can be altered by skillful and effective managers has contributed to a new view of the managers' job, roles, and requisite skills. The job of human service managers today is recognized as a proactive one, requiring leadership in the broadest sense as well as skills in the performance of a number of key managerial roles (Edwards & Yankey, 1991b). New and different approaches that are likely to be useful in preparing and guiding human service managers to manage their agency environments are being proposed (Schmid, 1992). Austin (1989) calls for "interactive leadership" to succeed in today's environment: managers should develop "political" skills to build and maintain effective linkage with external sources of legitimation and funding, and "cognitive" skills to analyze information about the environment which can then be used to guide the agency's future development. Increasingly, strategies are being offered that can be used by managers to maximize service effectiveness and organizational well-being in today's environment (Martin, 1987; Perlmutter, 1984).

Human service managers alone cannot deal with the pressures and demands from the environment. And just as the manager's job is being redefined in light of these realities, so the job of the direct service worker is similarly being re-examined. For example, the pivotal role that direct service workers play in spanning the agency's boundaries and scanning the environment is now appreciated. Workers frequently obtain valuable information about what is going on or what will happen in the environment from their relations and transactions with clients. When workers experience difficulties in providing services, they may be picking up early indications that their agencies are having problems with their environments. Formal and informal opportunities for workers to share their information, their insights, even in the preliminary stages when they may be little more than hunches, are essential.

As partners in their agency's survival, workers will find that they are expected to take seriously those aspects of their work that are important to powerful constituents. Mandated record-keeping and documentation if done unsatisfactorily can endanger an agency's operations. Participation in a number of activities which indicates compliance with laws and regulations, and thus demonstrates legitimacy and worthiness, takes on greater importance. We can now see that what workers do affects an agency's ability to acquire financial resources and foster community good will, and, ultimately, to attract and retain staff and clients.

Managers, attempting to steer their agencies through troubled times, need to count on workers who can be sensitive to their position and can recognize that managers are not necessarily the enemy of either staff or clients. More often, managers inherit policies and conditions that they must translate into agency regulations which have a negative impact on clients, workers, and service provision. Dealing with the agency's multiple constituents, they must spend an inordinate amount of time on inter-organizational relations, If they fail to do so, critical agency resources can be jeopardized.

Workers can be at the forefront, spearheading new and innovative programming, encouraging alternative structuring of services delivery, and supporting agency moves in different directions. Agencies that are flexible and can shift easily to accommodate changes in the environment not only survive, but continue to thrive in the long run (Herman & Heimovics, 1989). Although change is disconcerting, if not threatening, especially in times of uncertainty, unless provisions are made for easy adaptation, opportunities that may determine program and agency survival can be lost.

Workers are not being asked merely to go along with changes or program policies and procedures that result from environmental pressures and demands. Workers need to remain vigilant about the erosion of quality services, to stand up for their clients when necessary, and even to refuse to engage in work that they judge detrimental to the interests of clients. Managers may indeed be more responsive to the wishes, aims, and needs of their multiple constituents than to those of their own staff and clients. Despite their understanding of quality service, managers may not be able to withstand pressures of those who control critical resources (Martin, 1980). More than ever, managers need workers to uphold professional standards and identification to ensure quality services. And managers must buffer and protect workers from external pressures that interfere with workers' professional judgement and discretion. In the long run, agencies that maintain their commitment to the goal of high-quality service provision appear to best withstand assaults from the environment.

REFERENCES

Abend-Wein, M. (1991). Medicaid's effect on the elderly: How reimbursement policy affects priorities in the nursing home. *Journal of Applied Gerontology, 10*(1), 71–87.

Achenbaum, W. A. (1991). A brief history of foundation funding in aging. In B. R. Greenberg, I. A. Gutheil, L. M. Parker & R. H. Chernesky (Eds.), *Aging: The burden study of foundation grant-making trends* (pp. 17–29). New York: The Foundation Center.

Aldrich, H. (1979). *Organizations and environments*. Englewood Cliffs, NJ: Prentice-Hall.

Applebaum, R., & Phillips, P. (1990). Assuring the quality of in-home care: The "other" challenge for long-term care. *The Gerontologist, 30*(4), 444–450.

Austin, D. M. (1989). The human service executive. *Administration in Social Work, 13*(3/4), 13–36.

Austin D. M. (1991). Understanding the service delivery system. In R. L. Edwards & J. A. Yankey (Eds.), *Skills for effective human service management* (pp. 227–243). Silver Spring, MD: National Association of Social Workers.

Bailey, A. L. (1989, August 8). Big foundations giving more for specific programs, less for general support. *The Chronicle of Philanthropy*, pp. 4, 12, 13.

Biegel, D. E., Petchers, M. K., Snyder, A., & Beisgen, B. (1989). Unmet needs and barriers to service delivery for the blind and visually impaired elderly. *The Gerontologist, 29*(1), 86–91.

Capitman, J. A., Haskins, B., & Bernstein, J. (1986). Case management approaches in coordinated community-oriented long-term care demonstrations. *The Gerontologist, 26*(14), 398–404.

Cox, C., & Monk, A. (1990). Integrating the frail and well elderly: The experience of senior centers. *Journal of Gerontological Social Work, 15*(3/4), 131–147.

Edwards, R. L., & Austin, D. M. (1991). Managing effectively in an environment of competing values. In R. L. Edwards & J. A. Yankey (Eds.), *Skills for effective human services management* (pp. 5–22). Silver Spring, MD: National Association of Social Workers.

Edwards, R. L. & Yankey, J. A. (1991a). Managing organizational decline. In R. L. Edwards & J. A. Yankey (Eds.), *Skills for effective human services management* (pp. 204–216). Silver Spring, MD: National Association of Social Workers.

Edwards, R. L. & Yankey, J. A. (Eds.). (1991b). *Skills for effective human services management*. Silver Spring, MD: National Association of Social Workers.

Eggert, G. M., Friedman, B. & Zimmer, J. G. (1990). Models of intensive case management. *Journal of Gerontological Social Work, 15*(3/4), 75–101.

Estes, C. L. (1979). *The aging enterprise*. San Francisco: Jossey Bass.

Ewalt, P. L. (1991). Trends affecting recruitment and retention of social work staff in human services agencies. *Social Work, 36*(3), 214–217.

Foelker, G. A., Holland, J., Marsh, M., & Simmons, B. A. (1990). A community response to elder abuse. *The Gerontologist, 30*(4), 560-562.

Greenberg, B. R., Gutheil, I. A., Parker, L. M., & Chernesky, R. H. (1991). *Aging: The burden study of foundation grantmaking trends.* New York: The Foundation Center.

Gummer, B. (1988). The hospice in transition: Organizational and administrative perspectives. *Administration in Social Work, 12*(2), 31–43.

Gutheil, I. A., & Chernesky, R. H. (1991). Foundation support for aging in the 1990s: The emerging picture. *Journal of Applied Gerontology, 10*(1), 117–130.

Herman, R. D. & Heimovics, R. D. (1989). Critical events in the management of nonprofit organizations: Initial evidence. *Nonprofit and Voluntary Sector Quarterly, 18*(2), 119–132.

Hughes, S. L., & Guihan, M. (1989). Community-based long term care: The experience of the Living at Home programs. *Journal of Gerontological Social Work, 15*(3/4), 103–129.

IBM Funds Elder Care Projects (1991, April). *Gerontology News*, p. 4.

Kemper, P. (1990). Case management agency systems of administering long-term care: Evidence from the channeling demonstration. *The Gerontologist, 30*(6), 817–824.

Kerin, P. B., Estes, C. L., & Douglass, E. B. (1989). Federal funding for aging education and research: A decade analysis. *The Gerontologist, 29*(5), 606–614.

Kirwin, P. M. (1988).The challenge of community long-term care: The dependent aged. *Journal of Aging Studies, 2*(3), 255–266.

Krout, J. A., Cutler, S. J., & Coward, R. T. 1990). Correlates of senior center participation: A national analysis. *The Gerontologist, 30*(1), 72–79.

Levine, S., & White, P. E. (1961). Exchange as a conceptual framework for the study of interorganizational relationships. *Administrative Science Quarterly, 5*, 583–601.

Lombardo, N., & McConnell, S. (1990, February/March). The Alzheimer's Association's public advocacy success is rooted in family devastation. *The Aging Connection*, p. 10.

MacAdam, M., Capitman, J., Yee, D., Pottas, J., Leutz, W., & Westwater, D. (1989). Case management for frail elders: The Robert

Wood Johnson Foundation's program for hospital initiatives in long-term care. *The Gerontologist, 29*(6), 737–744.

Mahoney, C. W. (1989). *The role of foundations in aging: Grant making in an era of cost containment health policy.* Unpublished doctoral dissertation, University of California, San Francisco.

Martin, P. Y. (1980). Multiple constituencies, dominant social values, and the human service administrator: Implications for service delivery. *Administration in Social Work, 4*(2), 15–27.

Martin, P. Y. (1987). Multiple constituencies and performance in social welfare organizations: Action strategies for directors. *Administration in Social Work, 11*(3/4), 223–239.

Martin, P. Y., & O'Connor, G. G. (1989). *The social environment: Open systems applications.* New York: Longman.

Monk, A. (1990). Health care for the aged: The pursuit of equity and comprehensiveness. *Journal of Gerontological Social Work, 15*(3/4), 1–20.

Morris, R. (1989). Challenges of aging in tomorrow's world: Will gerontology grow, stagnate, or change? *The Gerontologist, 29*(4), 494–501.

Neugeboren, B. (Ed.). (1990). Coordinating human services delivery [Special Issue]. *Administration in Social Work, 14*(4).

Perlmutter, F. D. (Ed.). (1984). *Human services at risk: Administrative strategies for survival.* Lexington, MA: Lexington Books.

Perlmutter, F. D. (Ed.). (1988). Alternative social agencies: Administrative strategies [Special issue]. *Administration in Social Work, 12*(2).

Peterson, D. A. (1990). Personnel to serve the aging in the field of social work: Implications for educating professionals. *Social Work, 35*(5), 412–415.

Pfeffer, J. & Salancik, G. R. (1978). *The external control of organizations.* New York: Harper & Row.

Schmid, H. (1992). Executive leadership in human service organizations. In Y. Hasenfeld (Ed.), *Human services as complex organizations* (pp. 98–117). Newbury Park, CA: Sage.

Schreter, C. A. & Brummel, S. W. (1989). What foundations call funding opportunities. *Fund Raising Management, 20*(5), 32–39.

Seltzer, M. M., Krauss, M. W., Litchfield, L. C., & Modlish, N. J. (1989). Utilization of aging network services by elderly persons with mental retardation. *The Gerontologist, 29*(2), 234–244.

Stoesz, D. (1989). The gray market: Social consequences of for-profit eldercare. *Journal of Gerontological Social Work, 14*(3/4), 19–33.

Streib, G. F., & Binstock, R. H. (1990). Aging and the social sciences: Changes in the field. In R. H. Binstock & L. K. George (Eds.), *Handbook of aging and the social sciences* (pp. 1–16). New York: Academic Press.

Tolliver, L. P. (1988). The management of services to older Americans. In P. R. Keys & L. H. Ginsberg (Eds.), *New management in human services* (pp. 259–271). Silver Spring, MD: National Association of Social Workers.

Too few trained for aging work, reports contend. (1991, February). *NASW News*, p. 5.

Wernet, S. P., & Austin, D. M. (1991). Decision making style and leadership patterns in nonprofit human service organizations. *Administration in Social Work*, *15*(3), 1–17.

Wood, J. B. (1989). The emergence of adult day care centers as post-acute care agencies. *Journal of Aging and Health*, *1*(4), 521–539.

Zedlewski, S. R., et al. (1989). *The needs of the elderly in the 21st century*. Washington, DC: Urban Institute Press.

Afterword

Aging in the 1990s

Steven R. Gambert

PERHAPS ONE OF MAN'S GREATEST FEARS is to grow old, dependent, and ill. Although our species' maximum life span has
not changed since age of the cave man, the amount of time a
person can expect to live (the average life span) has steadily
increased, largely due to socioeconomic advances. Death
remains for most, however, something much more than the
natural end of life. Perhaps this is why so many claims have
been made promising miracle cures if only one would take
some elixir or perform some task. The truth is, aging is a
natural process from which no one can escape, and it affects
all cells, organs, and tissues in the body. A great deal of
confusion exists since we all "age" at different rates that are
determined largely by genetic and environmental factors.
But, in many cases, we unfortunately are guilty of accelerat-
ing our otherwise normal aging process. Things we do or fail
to do can cause us to be "older" or to perform less capably
than was genetically predetermined for us: a person who
smokes may have the lungs of an 80-year-old when he or she
is only 50 (!); sitting in the sun excessively will accelerate
the development of wrinkles in the skin; insufficient calcium
in the diet will cause us to lose precious minerals. Taking
these examples one step further: as the aging process accel-
erates, diseases may become more common. Smokers may
suffer bronchitis, emphysema, and even lung cancer as a
result. Skin cancer and osteoporosis are just two other examples of age-prevalent diseases that can largely be prevented.

In addition, many people stereotype the elderly. Merely
because people are of a certain age, they may be expected to
have certain problems or be unable to perform some task.

This has been referred to as "ageism," something as harmful as racism or sexism because it leads to prejudice and undesirable behavior. On the other hand, it is very common for an older person to blame some problem or discomfort on the aging process itself. Unfortunately, older persons often do have nonspecific symptoms of a disease, making it difficult even for the trained health care professional to diagnose a specific problem. The result is that problems are often diagnosed much later in their course and complications, which may have been prevented if caught earlier, may now result in a decline in functional capacity. This reduces the older person's ability to live independently. Because many age-prevalent diseases have no early signs or symptoms, screening programs have been advocated. For example, thyroid function testing, blood pressure checks, and blood sugar monitoring have been suggested for elderly persons or others thought to be at high risk of developing a specific problem.

Another aspect of prevention is immunization. Currently, we can prevent almost entirely influenza, pneumococcal pneumonia, and tetanus, among other killers. Surprisingly, thousands of persons die each year from these diseases because they fail to take proper preventive measures.

We are now faced with a growing population of older persons who pose a great potential burden for our health care system in the future. Although the elderly, those persons 65 years of age and older, comprise 12% of our nation's population, they will number 20% by the turn of the century, with the fastest growing number being those 80 years of age and older. This will have significant consequences as normal age-related changes continue to progress throughout life and result in even more loss of function. A critical loss in reserve capacity, often referred to as "homeostenosis," makes it more difficult for the older person to deal with a stressful life event, an adverse drug reaction, or an illness. In practical terms, whereas the younger person may survive an episode of hypotension or hypoglycemia with little sequellae, the older person may end with a stroke, myocardial infarction, or renal failure. Older persons are in the hospital more frequently and when hospitalized take longer to recuperate and return to the community. Persons aged 60 to 69 are hospitalized on a yearly average 3.0 days; persons aged 70–79, 4.7 days; and persons aged 85 and older, 8.3 days. Among elderly persons living in the community, approximately half receive ongoing treatment for arthritis, 30% have a significant hearing deficit, and 20% have a cardiovascular illness affecting their ability to conduct their usual activities of daily living. Almost half have some limitation in their physical functioning.

It is important to remember, however, that the current cohort of older persons did not have the knowledge we now have regarding the benefits of lifelong changes in lifestyle, diet, and exercise. Immunization programs were nonexistent when our senior citizens were young—we are looking at a class of survivors! Elderly persons living today have proved that they were not to die of childhood illness, heart attacks in their 50s, or colon cancer in their 60s. In fact, a 70-year-old woman can expect to live an additional 17.5 years; and a 70-year-old man, an additional 13.0 years. This has major ramifications when planning for one's future, whether it concerns retirement, finances, health, or family-planning.

Health care professionals must be cognizant of an older person's problems from a multidimensional perspective because not only will the older person experience physical limitations from illness and hospitalization, but he or she will also undergo a change in psychological outlook. Aging has been referred to as a "series of losses," and we must consider depression, frustration, and a high rate of suicide and alcoholism as factors when caring for the older, frail, and vulnerable person. In fact, elderly men who have become bereaved have the highest rate of new alcoholism and completed suicide of any age group. For this reason, a team of professionals is best suited to manage the complex and often interactive problems. Unfortunately, ways must be found to reimburse the time-consuming nature of geriatric care.

The current shortage of health professionals who are knowledgeable and willing to care for the elderly must be addressed from an educational, economic, and philosophical perspective. If we are to do justice to our elders and have as our goal for all to live their lives in the fullest and most productive manner, we all must begin to lobby for change. While the 1990s will most definitely bring much change to many, numerous challenges still need to be addressed. The geriatric imperative has never been more demanding!

ABOUT THE CONTRIBUTORS

Irene A. Gutheil, D.S.W., is an Assistant Professor at the Fordham University Graduate School of Social Service. She came to the academic world after many years of practice in the field of aging. At Fordham, she teaches in both the master's and doctoral programs and is the founder and Director of Fordham's Postgraduate Certificate Program in Gerontological Social Work. Her previous publications deal with issues in social work practice, the field of aging, and the physical environment and its impact on practice.

Martha C. Bial, M.S.W., is Associate Director of Field Instruction at the Fordham University Graduate School of Social Service. She received her bachelor's degree from Radcliffe College, her master's degree in Social Work from Columbia University, and is currently a doctoral candidate in Gerontological Social Work at Fordham University. As a hospital-based social work practitioner, she worked with neurologically impaired older people and their families, and for 15 years she was a social work consultant to six nursing homes.

Patricia Brownell, M.S.W., has worked in public sector social services for over 25 years. During this time, she has been involved in the research, planning, and project management for domestic violence and adult protective services programs, and community-based services for older people. She represents her agency on the steering committee of the New York City Coalition on Elder Abuse and is currently a doctoral candidate in Gerontological Social Work at Fordham University.

Roslyn H. Chernesky, D.S.W., Professor at the Fordham University Graduate School of Social Service, teaches administration and management, organizational behavior and the-

218 ABOUT THE CONTRIBUTORS

ory, program development, and proposal writing. As a director of training projects sponsored by the New York State Department of Social Services, she has prepared curricula and conducted statewide training in long-term–care systems management and comprehensive, community-based case management. In 1989, while a Postdoctoral Fellow in Applied Gerontology of the Gerontological Society of America, she completed a study (with Irene Gutheil) of grantmaking in aging, which was recently published by the Foundation Center in New York City.

Eileen R. Chichin, D.S.W., R.N., is Coordinator of the Kathy and Alan Greenberg Center on Ethics in Geriatrics and Long-Term Care at the Jewish Home and Hospital for Aged in New York City. As coordinator of a center in a long-term–care facility with both institutional and community-based programs, she collaborates with staff representing the professions of medicine, social work, nursing, nutrition, pharmacy, and occupational and physical therapy. Her educational background incorporates nursing, social work, and gerontology, and her previous publications have focused on the role of paraprofessionals in community-based long-term care.

Bart Collopy, Ph.D., is Associate for Ethical Studies at the Third Age Gerontology Center and Associate Professor in the Humanities Division of Fordham University at Lincoln Center. From 1987 to 1989, he was a Research Associate at the Hastings Center, a research institute studying ethical issues in medicine, health care policy, and related fields. His recent research has focused on ethical questions in health care for older people and on community-based care. He has written on these issues for several scholarly journals and has co-edited a recently published book on ethical issues in home care.

Elaine P. Congress, D.S.W., is an Assistant Professor at Fordham University Graduate School of Social Service where she teaches clinical practice, family-oriented treatment, and ethics to master's and doctoral level social work students, Formerly, she was Director of Social Work at the Sunset Park Mental Health Center of Lutheran Medical Center. She has published previously on cultural diversity in mental health practice and has in press an article on representative payee programs for older people.

Steven R. Gambert, M.D., F.A.C.P., is Professor of Medicine and Gerontology and Associate Dean for Academic Programs at New York Medical College. He has authored and co-authored more than 300 articles and has served in leadership positions in the Gerontological Society of America and the American Aging Association. Board-certified in Internal Medicine and Geriatric Medicine, he is a Fellow of the American College of Physicians, Gerontological Society of America, American Geriatrics Society, and New York Academy of Medicine.

Martha V. Johns, M.S.W., was Director of Member Services of the Federation of Protestant Welfare Agencies and Executive Director of the Jamaica Service Program for Older Adults. She is a candidate for a doctorate in Social Work and has a background in direct services to older people. A Brookdale Fellow, she is a member of the National Caucus and Center on the Black Aged, the National Association of Social Workers, the National Council on the Aging, and the Hunter College School of Social Work Alumni Association Board.

Ilse R. Leeser, Ph.D., R.N., is an Associate Professor at the Lienhard School of Nursing, Graduate Department, at Pace University in Pleasantville, New York. She is a family nurse practitioner at the Southeast Senior Center for Independent Living in Englewood, New Jersey, and has co-authored three textbooks dealing with nursing research, public health nursing, and primary care nursing.

Sally Robinson, D.S.W., has been Director of the City of Yonkers Office for the Aging since 1974. She received her master's degree in Social Work and post-master's certificate in Gerontology from the Hunter College School of Social Work and is currently a doctoral candidate at the Fordham University Graduate School of Social Service.

Barbara Silverstone, D.S.W., is the President of The Lighthouse Inc., the nation's most comprehensive vision rehabilitation agency, encompassing direct service, education, and research programs. Her numerous publications include three co-authored books: *You and your aging parent, Social work practice with the frail elderly and their families,* and the recently published *Growing older together: A couple's guide to understanding and coping with the challenges of later life.* Dr. Silverstone is a member of the National Association of Social Workers and Past President of its New York City Chapter, and a Fellow and Past President of The Gerontological Society of America.

Lynn M. Tepper, M.A., M.S., Ed.M., Ed.D., Director of the Institute of Gerontology at Mercy College in Dobbs Ferry, New York, coordinates the undergraduate gerontology specialization at Mercy College, and teaches graduate courses in adult development at Long Island University's campus at Mercy College. She also holds a clinical faculty appointment at Columbia University in the Schools of Public Health and Dental and Oral Surgery. A Fellow of the Gerontological Society of America, she was a delegate from New York to the last White House Conference on Aging.